Nigerian Cookbook

H. O. ANTHONIO
M. ISOUN

Macmillan

© H. O. Anthonio and M. Isoun 1982

All rights reserved. No reproduction, copy or transmission
of this publication may be made without written permission.
No paragraph of this publication may be reproduced, copied
or transmitted save with written permission or in accordance
with the provisions of the Copyright Act 1956 (as amended).
Any person who does any unauthorised act in relation to
this publication may be liable to criminal prosecution and
civil claims for damages.

Firsrt published 1982
Reprinted 1983, 1985

Published by *Macmillan Publishers*
London and Basingstoke
*Associated companies and representatives in Accra,
Auckland, Delhi, Dublin, Gaborone, Hamburg, Harare,
Hong Kong, Kuala Lumper, Lagos, Manzini, Melbourne,
Mexico City, Nairobi, New York, Singapore, Tokyo*

ISBN 0-333-32698-9

Printed in Hong Kong

Contents

Authors' Comments		iv
Introduction		vi
1	Kitchen Knowledge	1
2	Herbs, Spices, Seeds and Oils	15
3	The Staple Foods	29
4	Meat and Poultry	67
5	Fish and Shellfish	87
6	Land Snails	127
7	Vegetables and Salads	133
8	Simple Soups, Stews and Sauces	147
9	Milk, Cheese and Eggs	155
10	Small Chop, Snacks and Beverages	161
11	Desserts and Breads	177
12	Nutritionally Balanced Menus	199
Glossary		206
Related Reading		209
Table 1	Weights of Common Foodstuffs	210
Table 2	Quick Conversions	212
Table 3	Weight and Volume Conversions	213
Index		215

Authors' Comments

When I first came to Nigeria in 1965, an American friend showed me an article in a gourmet magazine written about the delights of the Nigerian food he had eaten in private homes in the Niger Delta. An article in the *New York Times*, however, gives the more typical response of visitors.

Eating in Black Africa, is, for most first time visitors, simply an unedifying necessity. The one thing the traveller will not find in Black Africa except in Ethiopia is local cooking in restaurants available to tourists. Since the cuisine relies heavily on starches and powerful doses of pepper, few regard its relative inaccessibility as any great loss. Some day Africans may develop enough pride in their own food to offer it commercially to their guests. However the first visit of a *Guide Michelin* inspector trained in the subtleties of pounded yam or bitter leaf stew is still a long way off.

While the first article confirmed my conviction that my enthusiasm for agbono soup and snails, and green plantain pottage was not misplaced emotionalism, the second kindled, out of annoyance, a commitment to bring the excellent and variable Nigerian cuisine back into more Nigerian homes and restaurants, as well as to the attention of the International community. When Mrs Anthonio and I were approached with the proposal that we write a Nigerian cookery book, we were both delighted and decided that, somehow, we would fit the project into our busy private and professional schedules. We have had to select recipes somewhat arbitrarily: the finished product is not a complete encyclopaedia; it could never be. However we hope it covers a cross section of recipes and increases written knowledge of Nigerian foods. We invite and will greatly appreciate additions, suggestions for improvement and other comments from readers so that subsequent editions can be both more comprehensive and helpful.

MIRIAM ISOUN

This book is written not only for students of catering but also for younger housewives interested in meal-planning and for the experienced housewife who is interested in newer and improved techniques in the art and technology of cooking.

Nigeria is a country with a very wide variation in food items, local seasonings, and tasty soups and stews. Unfortunately, there are very few records of these in book form. The possiblity of the disappearance of some food preparations is very real. It is, therefore, essential that the local catering techniques are well documented.

I am much indebted to my mother Mrs Henrietta Bolajoko Adeniyi, née Fagbohun, for providing me with the basics of catering prior to my formal education and professional career. I have inherited a lot from her, including the Brazilian-Lagos influence in catering, and innovations which she perfected during the early 1940s when she was the senior matron for Queen's College, Lagos.

I hope that this book will stimulate others to enlarge the printed knowledge of Nigerian foods.

H. OLAITAN ANTHONIO

Introduction

Nigerian food, as served in restaurants and at social functions generally, is limited to Jollof rice, moyin-moyin, oily meat and chicken stews and, perhaps, pounded yam and egusi soup. While these dishes are 'special occasion' foods for many Nigerians and are usually acceptable to and enjoyed by non-Nigerians, they become tiresome by their repeated appearance. Moreover, like foods in most cuisines, these dishes lose character and excellence when mass-produced. While the food in most Nigerian homes is more varied, housewives, like busy women everywhere, tend to shop for and cook a limited number of tried and familiar recipes, for convenience and economy. These same women, however, will recall, when encouraged to do so, many special foods prepared by their mothers and grandmothers. In most cases, the ingredients for these are still available, but time and the cost of preparation may be prohibitive.

When women from different parts of Nigeria discuss traditional foods and their preparation, two conclusions emerge:
a) there is a lot in common between one area of Nigeria and another;
b) there is a remarkable variation as well.

The authors feel that there is a need for a cookbook which introduces both Nigerians and non-Nigerians to the varied cuisine of Nigeria. Some Nigerians will find reminders of long forgotten dishes and want to reintroduce them into their diet. Others, particularly those raised in the urban areas, may be surprised to find their own foods can be used in different and interesting ways. Better utilisation of local foods can improve the nutritional quality of the diet because introduced foods are usually processed, thus removing valuable nutrients.

Finally, it is important to appreciate the variety, preparation and role of food as a part of traditional culture. Pride and care in the preparation of our own food specialities are as important as knowing how to perform traditional dances or wear traditional attire.

A Note To Non-Nigerian Readers

We hope that non-Nigerians, who may have the impression that culinary pleasures must be foregone while in Nigeria, will be encouraged to venture into the local markets and acquire a taste for the excellent and often unique foods to be found there.

For those living in other tropical countries, such as the Caribbean, the recipes in this book can provide new ways of using ingredients readily available to them. Europeans and North Americans can also find many of the ingredients in 'ethnic markets' and health food stores.

There are two characteristics frequently used to describe Nigerian foods; oiliness and hotness (from red pepper).

A quick glance through these recipes will reveal that only a few dishes are really 'oily'. These are often prepared for storage without refrigeration or for travelling. In other cuisines, proper use of large quantities of fats can give a desirable richness and texture, for example, Hollandaise sauce, butter cream frosting, not to mention the knob of butter often served on creamed (mashed) potatoes! Nigerians also have ways of incorporating fats in foods while cutting down on their oiliness. For example, the use of potash and special seed (agbono and ukpotoro) to 'homogenize' the oil, gives a richness rather than an unpleasant greasiness to foods.

There is also some misunderstanding about pepper-produced hotness. Firstly many people, for reasons of age, taste, health or family taboos, do not use hot pepper at all or only in very limited amounts. Secondly, red pepper can be incorporated into stews in ways that eliminate the hotness but leave the pleasant flavour of the pepper and the valuable vitamins it contains. Some dishes, of course, are changed drastically in character, colour, texture and flavour if the pepper is eliminated or reduced. This is especially true of dishes which contain uncooked fresh pepper, but the hotness can be reduced by removing the inner membranes and seeds before use. We suggest you increase the amount of pepper you use until it is not only tolerated but enjoyed, as it is a common ingredient, not only in Nigeria, but in many other tropical cuisines as well.

1

Kitchen knowledge

While this book is mainly a collection of tested recipes, the environment in which the cooking is done and the equipment used inevitably determine the quality of the product. It is for this reason that we have decided to include a few brief comments on the arrangement of kitchens, both traditional and modern, and on the equipment and utensils necessary for preparing the recipes included.

Traditional Kitchens

Traditionally, cooking areas are separate from the living quarters, being situated either in a different part of the same building or, more commonly, in a separate building. The equipment used is simple but functional. The stoves are of varying construction and burn firewood or charcoal. There is usually a hearth, or some hanging baskets over the cooking area, for drying and preserving foods. Utensils include knives and matchets, spoons (metal, wooden, calabash scoops, etc.), pots (iron and clay), basins (enamel, wooden, calabash, etc.), metal and woven strainers and baskets, graters of punctured metal and miscellaneous bottles and storage tins including vessels (usually of clay) for storing water. A mortar and pestle are invariably present, as are grinding stones.

Traditional Stoves

In addition to this 'standard' equipment, various speciality items may be present such as simple ovens of mud or metal drums.

While traditional kitchens are often functional, with some simple alterations they could be made more efficient and hygienic and thus more acceptable to today's housewife. Cooking and working areas are often low. By raising them, strain on the back is reduced and dangers to children are lessened. Foods and equipment are often stored on the floor but simple open shelves would help to keep these clean and handy. Kitchens are often dark and closed. Increased ventilation would make them more pleasant to work in and free of fumes and smoke. General cleanliness and brightness of walls, floors and equipment can easily be improved, even in the simplest kitchen, if a conscious effort is made to do so.

Modern Kitchens

In urban dwellings, there is a wide variety of kitchens. Many families share kitchens, others have private kitchens which are small and dark. The lucky ones have large, airy rooms to work in. In all cases, the suggestions given above for improving one's work situation can be applied to the urban kitchen as well. It is distressing to see in modern homes black walls and dirty floors,

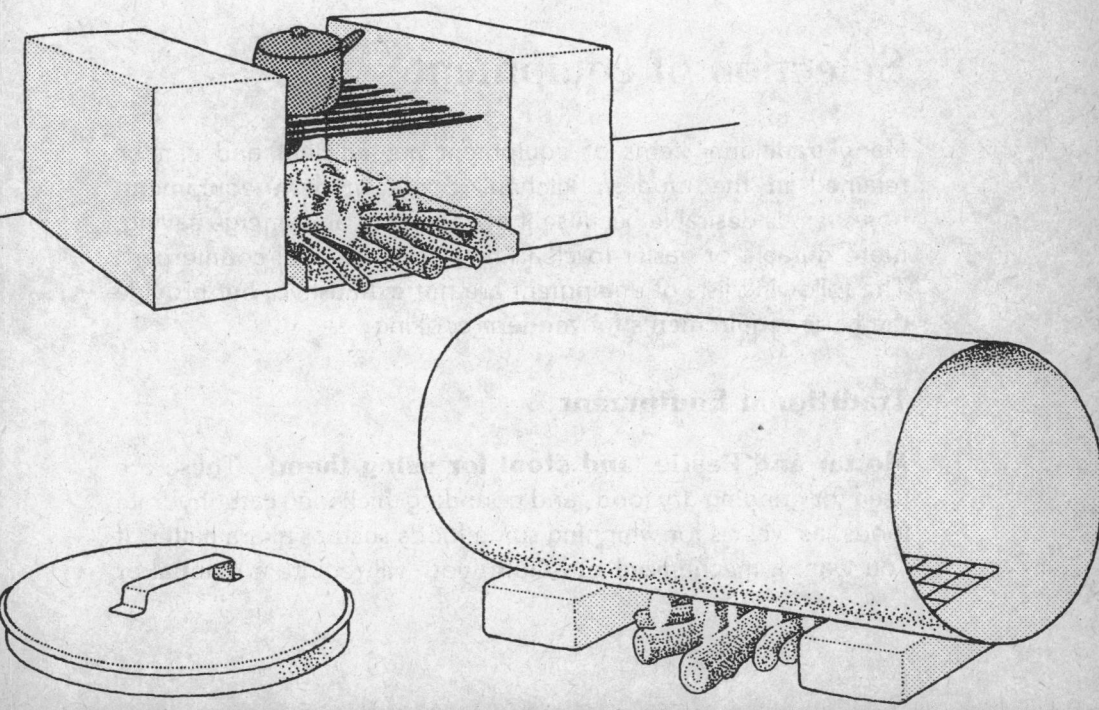

equipment stacked on floors, closets defaced with food and finger marks, as well as insects. Since we spend more time in our kitchens than we do in our sitting rooms, it is worth making the kitchen pleasant and clean so that our work will be a pleasure rather than a drudgery.

When considering changes in the kitchen, try to keep things simple. Keep in the kitchen only those things which are used regularly (special items can be stored). Keep shelves and cupboards immaculate: open shelves are preferable as one is more aware of their condition! Finish walls and shelves with a washable enamel paint and *wash* them regularly. Clean stoves and refrigerators inside and out regularly. It will lengthen their life and keep them hygienic. Keep food in clean containers suitable for maintaining freshness. Growth of moulds (fungi) and bacteria in foods is an ever-present and serious health problem in our climate. Fungi produce toxins in dry food which can cause both immediate and delayed diseases, so infected food should always be destroyed. Use large light bulbs. Mosquito net the windows so you can keep them open after dark. Avoid having unfinished wooden table tops as they will not dry properly and will harbour micro-organisms, even when washed. Plastic and metal surfaces are best. Arrange your equipment to save steps: the work table should be near the stove; the refrigerator near the sink; pots and pans stored near the stove, table ware near the dining area, etc.

Selection of equipment

Many traditional items of equipment are efficient and can be retained in the modern kitchen. Some modern equipment, however, is desirable because it may be time and energy saving, more durable or easier to clean than its traditional counterpart. The following lists of equipment are not exhaustive, but provide the basic requirements for modern cooking.

Traditional Equipment

Mortar and Pestle (and stool for using them) These are used for grinding dry foods and pounding thickened carbohydrate foods, as well as for whipping some foods such as akara batter. If you want a mechanized substitute, you will require a manual or electric mixer, a grinder, a blender and a mechanical yam pounder. With all these, you will still occasionally wish you had a mortar and pestle! Clean well with cold water and rinse with hot water between uses. Dry in the sun.

Grinding Stone This is used for grinding dry and wet foods. A blender and an electric food grinder can be substituted, but the flavour may be different.

Clay Pots Clay pots, locally produced, are ideal for reducing liquids because evaporation is facilitated by their shape and porous composition. There are many types available in different parts of the country. You should inquire from the local people as to their intended use. The more attractive ones can be used for cooking and serving as well. Clay pots are not very durable, but they are inexpensive.

Stove for Firewood or Charcoal Local stoves for burning charcoal and firewood are inexpensive, but their routine use makes it difficult to keep the kitchen clean and the pots get blackened by smoke. It is nice to have makeshift outdoor facilities, however, for charcoal roasting of foods and for special occasions. When large amounts of food are to be dried or steamed which are relatively fuel-expensive operations, these stoves are invaluable.

Modern Equipment

Stoves Kerosene cookers have an unpleasant smell and blacken the pots but are less expensive than other modern cookers. Those which require pumping to provide internal pressure can be dangerous. Gas cookers are clean, economical and efficient. They can, however, be dangerous and should never be used in closed kitchens or by children or uninformed adults. Be sure to store gas cylinders outside the kitchen and to turn them off every night. Leave windows open at night, if possible, to avoid build-up of fumes. Electric stoves are the safest, but are expensive to operate and inconvenient when the electricity supply is interrupted.

If you like to cook pastries, bake fish or meat, or reheat food in an oven, this can be purchased separately from the stove or as part of it. To save on fuel costs, be sure your oven is well insulated and try to bake with a full oven rather than with just one item. After baking, use the remaining heat for re-drying stored foods.

Large Basins Enamel, calabash and plastic basins are useful for soaking and washing dried and fresh fruits, and vegetables. They are also used for storing dried foods and for washing up.

Pots and Pans You will need several pots and pans of various sizes, with tight-fitting lids and heavy bottoms (thickened foods and stews will burn easily in pots with thin bottoms). Investment in good quality pots and pans will be worthwhile, as they will give decades of service.

Skillet A heavy-bottomed frying pan is necessary for frying eggs and some stews.

Steamer A large pot with a tight-fitting lid can be adapted for steaming, but if finances permit, a commercial or traditional steamer like the one shown here will be useful for Nigerian cookery, especially for foods wrapped in leaves.

Chopping Boards Two fine-grained heavy wooden boards of

convenient sizes are required. One for meats and strong-flavoured foods and another for fruits and breads (mild-flavoured foods). Always wash well and dry thoroughly between uses.

Graters There are convenient traditional graters of various sizes and shapes as well as commercially produced ones. You will need a fine one for citrus fruit peels and coconut and a coarse one for okro, ocoyam, etc. The native raspado, shown below, grates coconut without removing it from the shell.

Sieves You will need a sieve with large perforations (a colander) for draining vegetables. A fine one for sieving flour and preparing starches from carbohydrate vegetables is also useful.

Spoons You will need several spoons of different sizes and shapes. Metal ones (with and without perforations) and wooden ones are necessary. Calabash spoons and scoops are useful for serving. Long wooden 'flat' spoons are used for mixing thickened carbohydrate foods.

Knives Large and small knives and a matchet, all of which can be easily sharpened, are required. Using a stone for sharpening is better than relying on a cement doorstep or ceramic sink as many

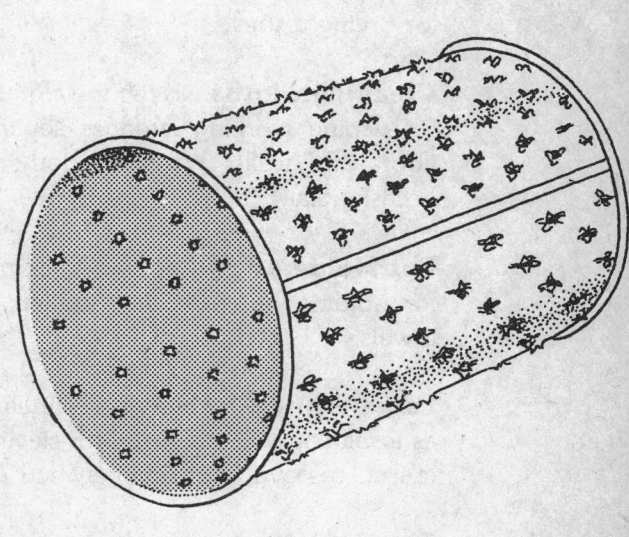

Steamers and Graters

housewives do. Some knives should be stainless steel for use with acid-containing foods, although these knives do not hold their edges well.

Trays These are needed for drying foods in the sun and for efficiency in moving kitchenware about.

Cooling Racks Cooling racks for baked and steamed foods and for resting hot pots, are available in both traditional bamboo and modern metal forms.

Refuse Containers These should be easy to clean. They should be emptied and cleared daily. Line with newspaper to facilitate cleaning.

Baskets Plastic and cane baskets are useful for storage of fresh foods.

Airtight Tins, Bottles, Jars A variety of containers is needed for storage of dry foods, oils and spices, and for the refrigeration of cooked and partly processed foods. Covered water storage containers are essential in most localities.

Towels and Towel Rod These items should be located next to the sink so that regular handwashing becomes a habit for all members of the family. Use separate towels for drying hands and for drying dishes.

Cleaning Cloths Keep the cloths used for washing dishes and for wiping working surfaces separate from those for cleaning floors and walls. Wash all cloths regularly and sun dry. Boil occasionally.

Pot Holders Make some thick mats of several layers of cloth for holding hot pots and spoons. They are much safer than towels.

Large White Cloth Bag A finely woven clean cloth bag, such as a salt bag, will be useful for sieving starch suspensions such as maize, cassava, etc. Boil between uses.

Standard Measuring Containers For this book you need

metric scales for weights and a millilitre-marked container for volume. Alternatively use the Handy Measure containers shown on pages 12 and 13.

Can Opener Select a tin opener that leaves the edges of the tin smooth. It is safer to use and the opened tins are less likely to cause injuries.

Egg Whisk or Rotary Beater A manual or electric mixer to incorporate air into food mixtures is necessary. For some foods, such as ewedu, a whisk of local broomsticks can be used.

Baking Tins If you like to prepare baked goods, select a few versatile tins. If possible get heavy aluminium or stainless steel; the tins will last many years and the baked products will look nicer.

Modern Conveniences

Refrigerator with a Freezing Compartment The most convenient means of preserving fresh and cooked moist foods is in a refrigerator. Fresh meats and fish should be deep frozen unless used immediately. Follow the manufacturer's instructions for regular defrosting and cleaning to prolong the life of this substantial investment.

Deep Freeze A deep freeze allows one to buy meat, fish, poultry and even baked goods in quantity when prices are low. For the working wife, advance preparation of cooked foods is a convenience. Soups and stews without a boiled carbohydrate or carbohydrate thickener freeze well. Cooked vegetable greens, okro, puréed tomato, onion and pepper all freeze well. Be sure to date all items stored, as nothing keeps indefinitely. In Nigeria, where current may fluctuate, it may be worthwhile protecting the compressor with an automatic circuit breaker. Follow the manufacturer's instructions on maintenance carefully.

Pressure Cooker A pressure cooker saves time and fuel costs when cooking meats and boiled carbohydrates such as beans, rice, and maize. It can be used as a steamer. Always use carefully according to the manufacturer's instructions as pressure cookers can be dangerous if used incorrectly.

Food Grinder There are many types of food grinders, each with different potential. A small electric coffee grinder is most useful for grinding daily portions of egusi seeds, dry crayfish, spices and finely chopped agbono. There are manual food mills for preparing flour from dried carbohydrate foods or purée from wet ones. Heavy-duty motorised models are available in the markets; for a few kobo, you can grind soaked maize or beans, or dry rice or yam.

Blender (Liquidizer) A simple blender or liquidizer if used carefully according to the manufacturer's instructions will make the cooking of Nigerian foods much simpler and will give years of service. Most models require the contents to be more or less liquid. Tomatoes, onions and soaked cowpeas can be puréed; greens and okro can be chopped finely. Some models will also grind dry foods, but knives dull quickly and replacement parts are not always available.

Deep Fryer with Basket This is a handy piece of equipment which ensures that all food fried in a batch can be removed at the same time. It is safer than draining individual products with a fork or spoon.

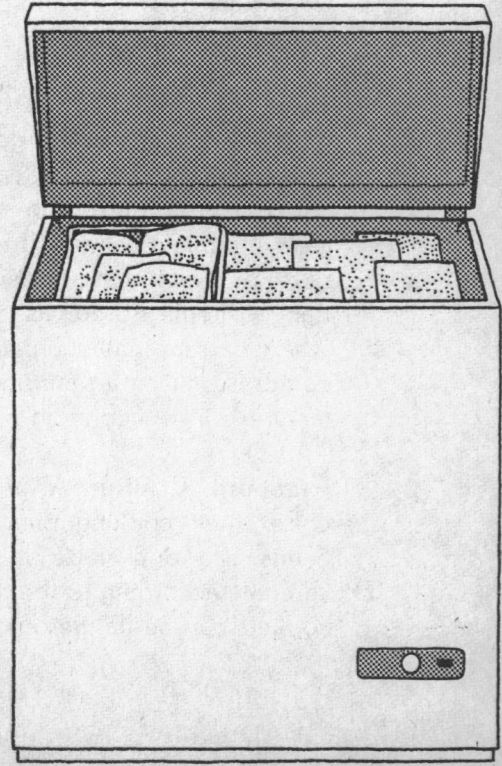

KITCHEN KNOWLEDGE   11

Use of Recipes

Recipes as such are not part of traditional cookery techniques in Nigeria and the ingredients used in most dishes are not absolute. However, it is difficult to cook any kind of food without having seen it prepared or having eaten it previously, unless exact directions are given. Every recipe included in this book has been tested. Therefore, by following the recipes, it should be possible for anyone to prepare recognisable Nigerian dishes. Once a dish has been successfully cooked, however, individual variation is both desirable and rewarding.

To cook good Nigerian food, one must be prepared to buy the best quality foods and these will often be expensive. This is true, of course, of food anywhere. However, with careful planning and adjustment of recipes, it is possible to cater well and economically. For this reason we have included comments on marketing and storing of food and also menu suggestions.

In order to provide a more complete cookery book for the cook in Nigeria, we have included a few selected 'introduced' recipes. These recipes are clearly marked as such and were selected for one or more of the following reasons:

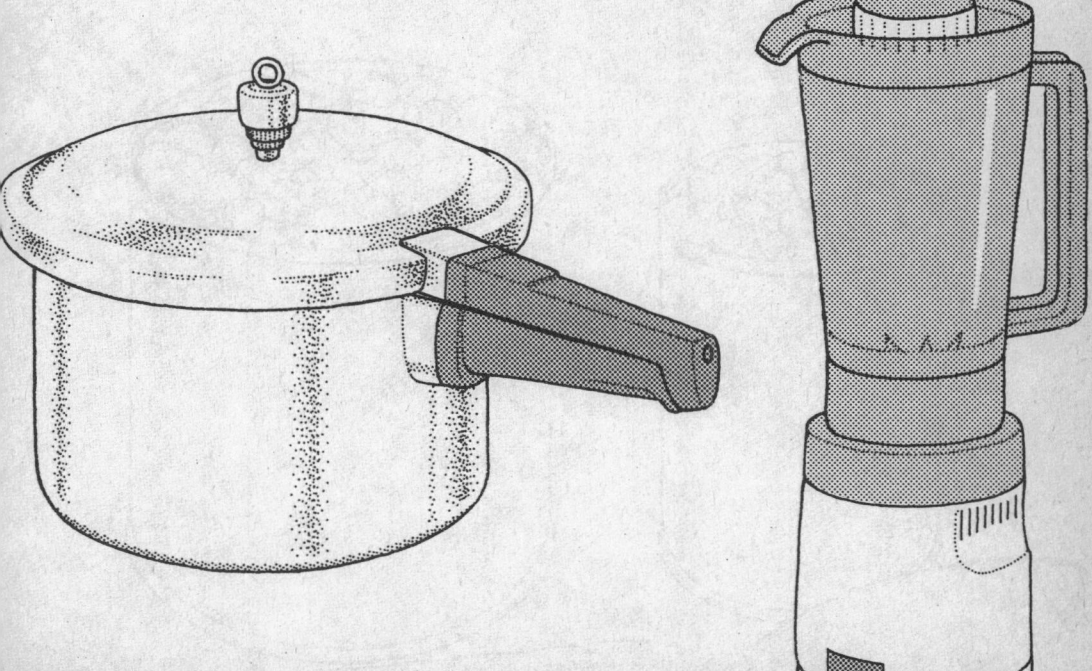

Modern Kitchen Equipment

1 They use local foods in new ways.
2 They have been found by experience to be generally acceptable to Nigerian tastes.
3 They use readily available foods conveniently or economically.

Some of our limited choice of pastries and cakes, for example, use imported wheat (flour), but others use local flours, oils and flavourings.

Weights and Measures

Because standard measurements are not commonly used in most Nigerian kitchens, a convenient but accurate system of measuring had to be developed. Although there are typical measuring containers used in the market, such as the milk tin, muda, congo, and kerosene tin, the actual volume measured out varies because similar containers vary in size and the contents may be level or, more commonly, heaped. One occasionally sees spring scales being used by meat and vegetable sellers. Unfortunately these, too, are prone to inaccuracy and manipulation. Most housewives do not have the scales used by British cooks or the measuring cup used by Americans. Instead they have a collection of spoons and

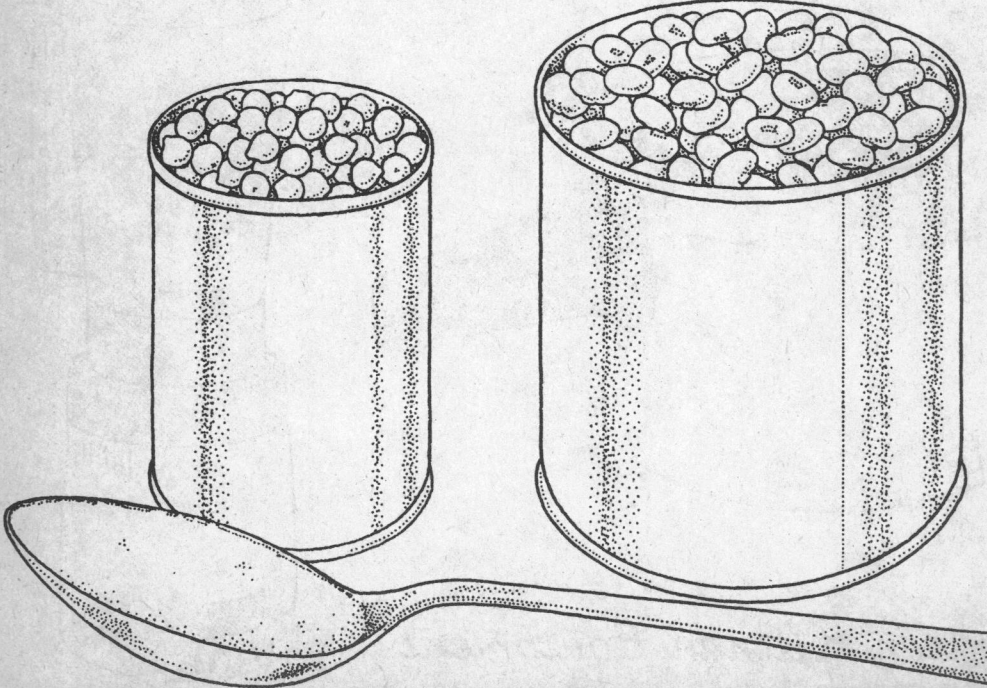

cups from around the world, all varying in volume. We, therefore, decided to base all our measurements on a few available spoons and containers which could be readily assembled by the cook for regular use. We have called these Handy Measures. In addition, because most of the world is adopting the metric system, we have included the metric equivalent with each recipe. If one wishes to convert these two systems (Handy Measure or Metric) into a more familiar system (British pounds and ounces or American cups and tablespoons, for example), Table 2 at the end of the book can be consulted. There are many ingredients, such as fresh tomato, fresh pepper or greens, which cannot conveniently be measured in volume. We have described these as small, medium or large but if variation is likely to affect the outcome of the recipe, the chopped or sliced volume and the actual metric weight is given.

Another problem arises when listing ingredients and giving the names of recipes. There are over three hundred different languages and a multiple of that number of dialects in Nigeria. Each language and often each dialect will have a specific name for each type of pepper, yam and leaf. English is the national language at present, but many of our foods are not known by the English names and these would not be useful in the markets. On the other hand, English names which are not always used in the British English way, or are part of Pidgin English, may be in

Handy Measures

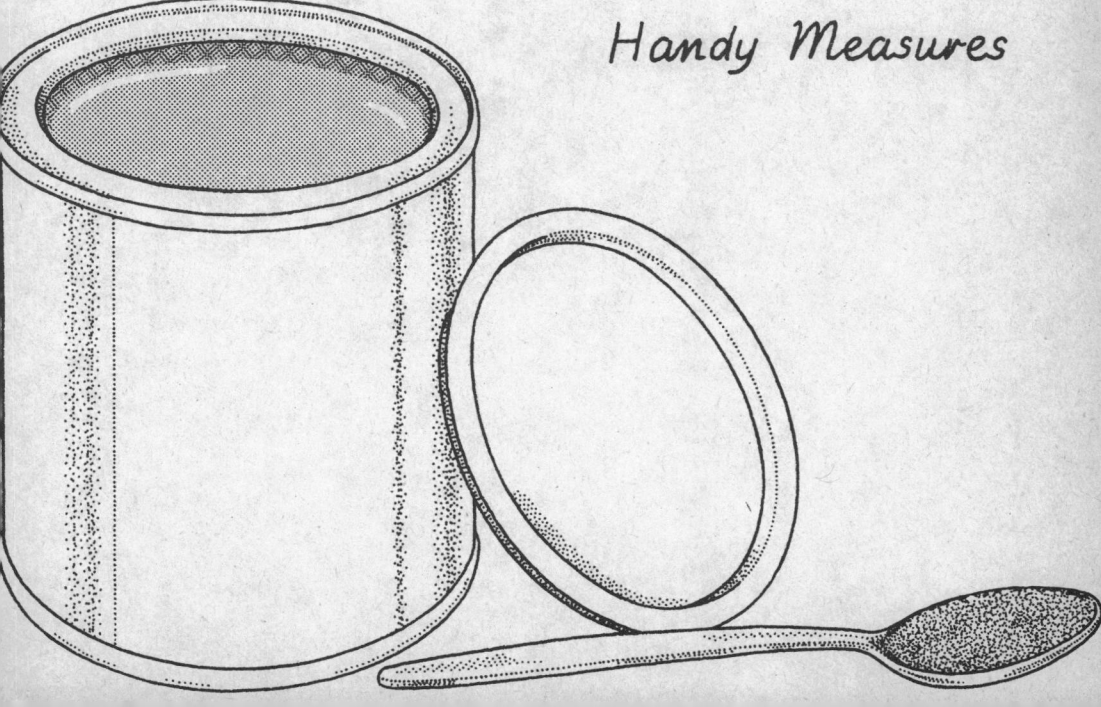

common use. Such terms are often described as being 'Nigerian English'. It is most useful to be able to use these adaptations and terms correctly in the Nigerian context, so some of the more common terms are included in the glossary. For example, when the term 'beans' is used in the market, one is usually referring to cowpeas, either the brown variety, or the 'black-eyed peas' of the southern United States.

In cases where the English equivalent of an ingredient is not available or useful, a Nigerian language equivalent had to be selected. In general, we have used the word we feel will be most widely understood. For example, *tatasai* is used throughout Nigeria in cooking, and although each language will have its own word for this specific pepper, the Hausa word *tatasai* is generally recognised, at least in urban markets. In the section on spices and herbs, the name used throughout the book will be given along with selected other languages from areas where the food may also be commonly in use. The glossary will also be helpful in the identification of foods in different languages, although no attempt has been made to make this comprehensive.

2

Herbs, spices, seeds and oils

Regional differences in basically similar dishes frequently depend on the variety of spices and flavourings available. While dried seeds, roots and herbs may provide this variety, the addition of fermented seeds, special oils and seeds with special properties such as thickening and 'draw' can also alter flavour and texture dramatically. In addition, they can give increased nutritional value to the dish.

Names Used in Recipes

1 *Seed and Root Spices (usually dried)*
   African nutmeg   Ginger
   African black pepper   Rigije
   Atariko   Ukpotoro
   Emilo   Yanghanyanghan
   Enge
   Gbafilo
   Turmeric

2 *Red peppers (used fresh and dried)*

3 *Herbs (usually fresh)*
   African lemon grass   Bitter leaf
   Afzelia bella bella   Tea-bush
   Beletientien   Partminger

4 *Miscellaneous Flavourings*
   Dry crayfish   Potash
   Dried okro   Orange peel

5 *Oils and Fats*
   Butter   Palm oil
   Chicken oil   Salted pork oil
   Coconut oil   Soybean oil
   Corn oil   Vegetable oils
   Egusi-seed oil   Vegetable shortening
   Fish oil   (solid)
   Ghee
   Groundnut oil
   Margarine

6 Seeds
   Agbono   Locust bean
   Coconut   Oil beans
   Egusi   Sesame seed (Benne-
   Groundnuts   seed)

Seed and Root Spices

African Nutmeg: *Monodora myristica* (Ijaw: *arigo*; Ibo: *ehuru*; Itsekiri: *iwo*; Yoruba: *ariwo*: Hausa: *gujiya-dan-miya*) These seeds, which are obtained from inside a large round fruit, are dried for marketing. When purchased, the seed should be opened and the inner serrated nut removed. This may be roasted over an open flame for a few seconds or used directly. Grind in a mortar or with a stone. A large quantity may be ground in a blender. The ground spice should then be stored at room temperature if well dried or in the refrigerator. In the Delta and surrounding areas, the African nutmeg may be bought at food stalls; in some other areas it is more easily found in the medicine or cosmetic sections of the markets. It is especially good in pepper soups, pottages, and with shrimp. It can also be used as a painkiller, a linament and as a scent in cosmetics.

African Black Pepper: *Piper nigrum* (Yoruba: *iyere*; Efik: *ada*; Ibo: *oziza*) Small black seeds dried for marketing. Grind before adding to any soup or stew to taste. It is much like the ground black or white pepper of Europe and America.

Atariko (Itsekiri) Small seeds sold in, or removed from, an alligator pepper-like pod. Highly scented, but not as hot as alligator pepper. It is expensive so use only a few of the tiny seeds to flavour pepper soups, or banga soup with rigije. Sold in the markets by traders from the Delta areas.

Enge (Ijaw): *Xylopia aethiopica* (Itsekiri: *egidije*; Yoruba: *eeru* Efik and Ibibio: *atta*; Ibo: *uda*; Hausa: *kimba*: Igalla: *alu*) Clusters of long black seed pods, more or less constricted between internal seeds. The long pods are broken in several places or crushed so that the flavourful seeds are broken. Use in pepper soups and other dishes. Remove the pod before serving.

Gbafilo (Itsekiri) Large, egg-shaped seed with rough sandpaper-like surface. The nut, which shakes freely inside, is removed and ground for inclusion in pepper soups. Sold in the markets by traders from the Delta areas.

Turmeric: *Curcuma longa* (Common name: red ginger; Hausa: *gangamau*) Root used dry for spice, especially in introduced curries. Also used for dye, cosmetics (eye make-up) and medicine (vermifuge, jaundice treatment, eyewash and ointment for skin diseases).

Ginger: *Zingiber officinale* (Common name: white ginger; Yoruba: *atale*; N Nigeria: *chittafo*) The root is used fresh or dried and ground for spice on meats, in moyin-moyin and in chicken dishes. Also used medicinally for catarrh, toothaches, neuralgia.

Rigije (Itsekiri) Small brown flat seeds used with atariko in banga palm fruit pulp soups. Sold by Delta market women.

Ukpotoro (Ibo): *Mucuna flagilipes* (Yoruba: *ise*; Efik: *ibaba*) Black flattened seed with two grey stripes. The seed is shelled, boiled for thirty minutes and pounded with a small amount of oil before being added to okazi vegetable soup where it provides a mucilaginous binding quality. Shelled, boiled and fermented, it can be slivered and substituted for oil bean.

Yanghanyanghan (Itsekiri) *Tetrapleura tetraptera* (Efik: *uyayak*) These long wing-bean shaped pods are sold dried in

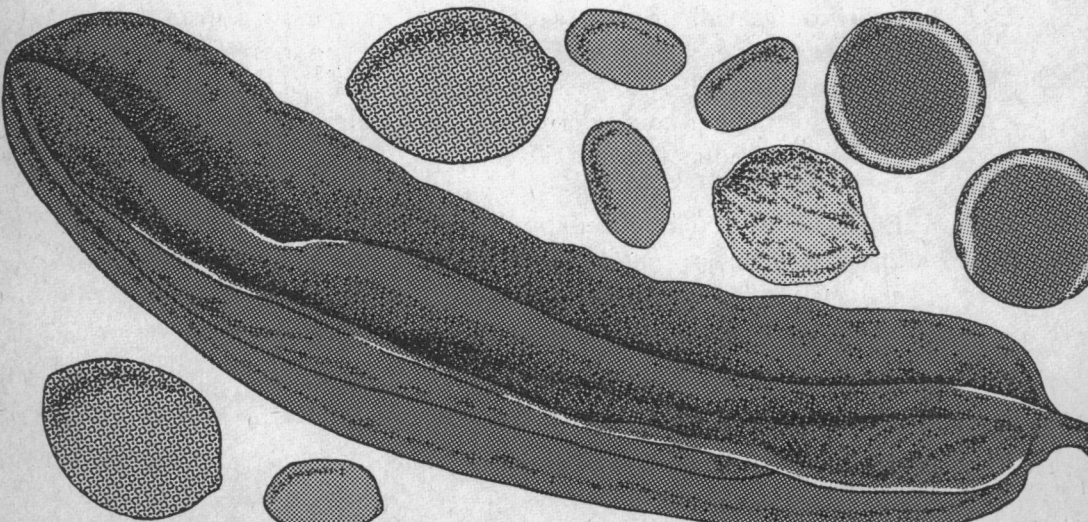

the market by Delta women for spice and in other locations for spice, cosmetics or dyes. Remove the inner soft portion from the 'wings' when dry and use ground in pepper soups.

Red Peppers

Many varieties of red peppers (*Capsicum*), both fresh and dried, are available all year round in the market. Dry pepper is sold whole or ground and is used mainly to give hotness. Fresh pepper gives flavour, colour, thickening and hotness to foods. The seeds and membranes, which are irritating to the skin and some digestive systems, may be removed before being used raw or cooked. Names for the most common types given below were selected because they are widely understood in urban markets.

Ata wewe Small, very hot pepper which is usually dried.

Sombo Long, small pepper which is usually dried. Not as hot as *ata wewe*.

Ata rodo: *Atanla* Medium-sized red pepper which is usually used fresh. Provides flavour, hotness and thickens the stew.

Tatasai Large 'sweet' red pepper which provides flavour and thickening. Not very hot, particularly if the seeds and membranes are removed.

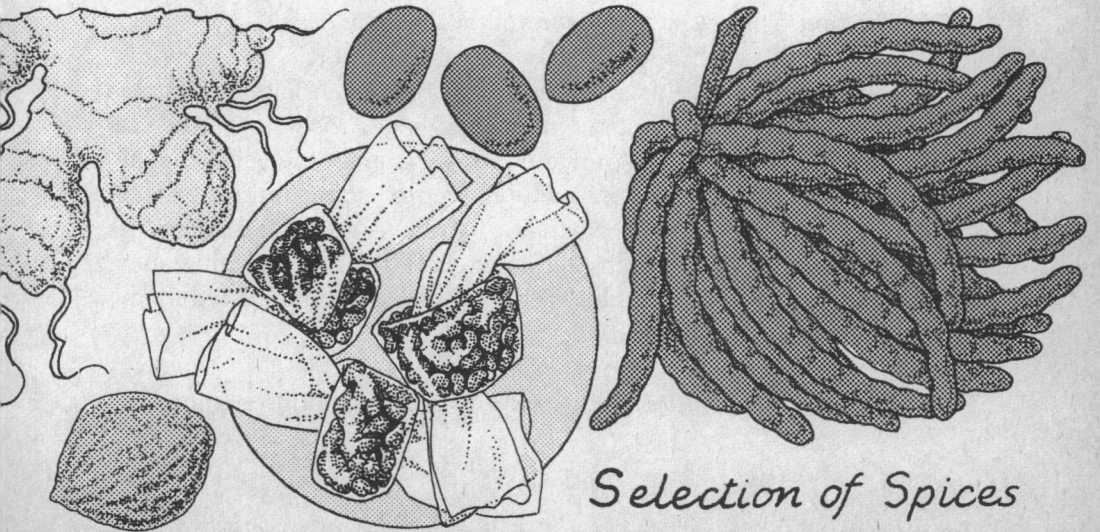

Selection of Spices

Herbs

African Lemon Grass: *Cymbopogon citratus* (Yoruba: *koko oba*; Ibo: *achara ehi*; *akwukuo*; Efik: *ikonti*: Ibibio: *myoyaka*) Easily cultivated. Used for making tea and in some Delta pepper soups and pottages. Also a local deterrent to tsetse fly and snakes.

Afzelia Bella Bella (Ibo: *ule ule*) The fermented leaves of this plant can be purchased from Eastern market women. They are added to boiling yam to give aroma and flavour.

Beletientien (*Itsekiri*) This herb is usually purchased dried and ground from women from Bendel State in the local markets. Sprinkle over palm-nut soup when cooking.

Bitter Leaf: *Vernonia anyadalina* (Yoruba: *ewuro*; Efik: *etido*) This large shrub, which only grows in the tropics, is botanically related to lettuce, chicory and daisies. To remove most of the bitterness in the leaves, they are usually crushed and washed thoroughly. Bitter leaf is easily grown and is also readily available in the market either as fresh leaves or washed and scrubbed. It can also be dried for storage. Bitter leaf is used as a vegetable in stews, often with egusi. It gives a bitter, mildly astringent quality to the dish. It is also widely used medicinally. (The file powder used in gumbos in Louisiana, U.S.A. is a herb mixture based on sassafras, which appears to have been adopted as a substitute by Africans there). Another plant used to produce the same effect as bitter leaf in many parts of the East is the climbing plant, *Crongronema ratifolia* (Ibo: *utazi-zi*).

Tea-bush and Partminger The botanical family *Labietae* includes thyme, oregano, marjoram, sage, rosemary, lavender and others. These are pungent herbs, several of which are available and used in Nigeria. Two of the more widely popular are tea-bush and partminger. Neither of these is usually seen in the market, as they are both readily grown from seed and may even be found as weeds. If they are not available, fresh or dried thyme or basil may be substituted.

Tea-bush: *Ocimum gratissimum* (Yoruba: *efinrin*; Benin: *ihiri*;

Efik: *mfang, amana*; Ibo: *'nchaawu*; Kalabari: *akeni*, Kolokuma: *furuegena*)   The fresh leaves are used in a wide variety of ways. In the Delta they are used in pepper soups and pottages; in Kwara for egusi soups; in Igalla as a vegetable; and in other places, raw in salads. These leaves are widely believed to aid digestion.

In case of nose bleeds, apply the crushed leaves, to stop the blood flowing.

Partminger *Ocimum canum* (Nigerian common name: curry leaf; American: basil, mint)   Use as tea-bush.

Miscellaneous Flavourings

Dried Crayfish   Dried crayfish (actually dried shrimp) is used in soups and stews mainly as a flavouring. It also provides valuable nutrients, especially protein. It is convenient to buy in bulk as dry crayfish must be picked over to remove foreign objects and re-dried in the sun or a 225°F, 110°C oven. Small dried crayfish are usually used ground; larger ones may be used whole, after removing the heads, tails and legs. The removed parts can be ground and added to food as well. Grinding can be done in a mortar, on a stone, in a coffee grinder or in a blender. Store whole or ground. Keep very dry in an airtight container.

Dried Okro (Hausa: *nuru*; Yoruba: *orunla*)   Dried okro is sold in the market sliced or ground. It can also be prepared at home by slicing thinly and sun-drying fresh okro. When pounded or ground, it is added to soups for a flavour different from fresh okro, and for thickening.

Potash   Kaun and native salt are forms of potash prepared locally. They are used for flavouring and to shorten the cooking time of some foods. Some foods are changed in colour when potash is used. Kaun is sometimes used to keep palm oil from separating from the water in stews. Available in all markets.

Orange Rind, Grated   Orange rind can be used in sweets to give a natural fresh flavour. Grate the outermost oily surface of the orange finely, without including the underlying white bitter membrane. Use one teaspoon grated orange rind as a substitute for one teaspoon vanilla flavour in any recipe. (Lemon rind can be prepared in the same way).

Oils and Fats

Nigerians use a wide variety of oils and fats in their cooking as ingredients for soups and stews and for frying. The most popular are palm oil and groundnut oil. The supply of both of these oils does not meet present demand, so many other cooking fats and oils are now available in the local markets.

Butter Butter is imported and is expensive. As it is perishable, it is sold only in shops. Butter as a table spread is an acquired taste in Nigeria: perhaps one best not acquired!

Chicken Oil A special oil prepared in the home. The fat, which rises to the top of the broth from well-seasoned boiled chicken or pepper soup, is skimmed off and stored in a cool place for a few days. It is used for serving on boiled vegetables such as yam, cocoyam or green plantain. It is also nice for preparing omelettes.

Coconut Oil Coconut oil can usually be located in large urban markets and in smaller markets near its source. It is sold both as a body oil and for consumption. Try it in Jollof rice or coconut rice and use it as cooking oil in baking (use about ten per cent less oil when substituting for a solid shortening such as butter). Coconut oil, like animal fats, contains mainly saturated fatty acids and becomes rancid unless stored in a cool place or an airtight container. Buy in small quantities.

Corn Oil Imported and expensive. Use as for vegetable oil.

Egusi-seed Oil A special oil produced locally. Occasionally it can be seen tinned commercially. Used in stews and on boiled foods.

Fish Oil A special oil produced in the home when frying or drying oily fish. Very nutritious. This is definitely a seasonal localised delicacy and is sometimes given as a gift. Served with boiled foods such as yam and green plantain.

Ghee (Clarified butter) or *'ghee substitute'*. Imported for the Asian community. Sometimes seen in the local market where it is prized for frying plantain. Can be used as other vegetable oils but has a unique butter-like taste which may not be desirable in many local dishes.

Groundnut Oil Nigeria produces excellent groundnut oil. While groundnut oil has excellent nutritive value, it has been largely replaced by the cheaper vegetable oils in the market. It has a distinctive groundnut smell, but this can be driven off by heating if it is not desirable in the finished product. High in unsaturated fats.

Margarine Many imported and locally produced varieties of margarine are available. Tinned margarine is available even in the local markets, although packets and tubs of soft margarine are sold in the larger shops. Used mainly on bread. Tinned and packet margarine can be used in baking.

Palm Oil The fruits of the oil palm are used in food, mainly as a source of refined oil. The husked fruits are also used fresh by extracting and sieving the unrefined oil-containing pulp to prepare banga soups. The palm kernel within the remaining hard, thick-shelled nut is also eaten as snack food. The nut should be dried for a few days in the sun to facilitate the removal of the inner nut-meat.

The whole palm fruit, as harvested, can be purchased from local farmers or it can be bought in smaller quantities, husked, in the markets. Palm fruit should not be stored for more than a few days, but can be boiled for ten minutes, cooled and frozen. Alternatively, the pulp can be prepared and frozen.

Palm oil contains vitamins not present in most refined oils and is, therefore, an important ingredient in many soups and stews. It comes in several different grades. The most expensive and difficult to find is made for table use. It is flavoured with coconut and spices during extraction according to local tastes and is served uncooked with boiled foods such as yam or green plantain. It can also be used in the preparation of uncooked sauces. This oil is not readily available in the local market, but if you make friends with a market woman who buys palm oil at source, she may be able to get some for you. The palm oil processed in the eastern states is generally considered superior to that processed in the large commercial oil mills throughout the country. However, the selection of good oil is always best made by tasting it before buying it. Good oil will not coat the tongue and will not be bitter or strong smelling. It will be bright red, rather than too dark in colour; it may be oily, thick or almost solid. The oil sold in the supermarkets in tins is not as good as good oil from the market, but this oil and inferior market oil can be improved if some onion is fried in it — the heating drives off some unpleasant scent and the onion imparts some additional flavour.

It should be emphasised that *good* market palm oil is tasty. It can be eaten without cooking, can be used directly without frying in stews and will not give an unpleasant odour or taste to the product.

Salted Pork Oil Similar to chicken oil, but prepared from salted pork.

Soybean Oil Soybean oil has many nutritional advantages, but, unfortunately, is not commonly available yet in Nigeria. It is sometimes a constituent of the 'vegetable' oils seen in the markets.

Vegetable Oils Five-gallon tins, one-gallon tins, and unlabelled bottles of 'vegetable' oil are sold in every local market. They are increasingly being used as substitutes for palm oil and groundnut oil in most foods. These oils, locally produced or imported from around the world, usually do not state the type of seed from which the oil was extracted. Unfortunately, much of the vegetable oil being sold in Nigeria today is refined and bleached palm oil. This palm oil has been exported from the tropics, and imported again in a less nutritious form. Other 'vegetable' oils consist of any one or a blend of a wide variety of oils such as corn, groundnut, cottonseed, and soybean oils. Vegetable oils please the housewife as they are tasteless, relatively colourless and do not 'splatter' when heated, unlike the more familiar groundnut and palm oils. For frying, these qualities make vegetable oils particularly attractive but for regular incorporation in soups and stews, good nutrition dictates the continued use of the less processed, locally produced oils.

Vegetable Shortening (Solid) A variety of solid vegetable shortenings is available. These appeal to the cook as they can be kept at room temperature and can be used for frying as well as baking. They are generally tasteless and white in colour.

Seeds

Many seeds are used in Nigerian cooking. They are generally used ground, and provide special flavours, thickening and often add oil to the dish. Such seeds are important nutritionally as they contain vitamins, minerals and substantial quantities of plant protein.

The seeds described below include those in recipes in this book. There are many more seeds used seasonally in particular areas. Cowpeas, a most important component of Nigerian foods, are seeds, but are discussed in Chapter 3, The Staple Foods.

Agbono: *Irringia gabonsis* (Common name: wild or African mango, bush mango) The fruits of the bush mango tree are opened and the seeds split to remove and dry the inner nuts (agbono) before marketing. The agbono is very hard and is always ground before use as a flavouring and thickening in soups. It gives a more or less mucilaginous 'draw' to the soup depending on how the dish is prepared. Before grinding, the darker coloured hard-back of the nut can be removed, but this removes some nutrients and is not necessary. Grinding can be done in a mortar or on a stone by adding some oil, or in a machine in the market. It can also be ground in a blender or coffee grinder *if cut into small pieces first*, but it is difficult to get it as fine as is usually required. It may help to chill the chopped nuts first before using a blender. Although the final product may taste slightly different, the coarsely broken agbono can be boiled in water or stew to soften before being blended and then returned to the soup. Agbono is very nutritious because it contains a large amount of oil (10 per cent), protein (31 per cent) and vitamins. Agbono is popular throughout Nigeria, although in a few localities it is considered taboo.

Coconut: *Cocos nucifera* The coconut is the seed of the coconut palm. Coconut is fairly rich in protein and oil, but contains mainly cellulose and readily digestible sugars.

Coconut meat is used as a snack or in combination with other foods as a light meal. For example, fresh coconut is served with soaked garri or roasted fresh corn. The coconut milk extracted from the meat is used in baking and in rice dishes and curries.

To buy Buy fresh coconuts which feel heavy and contain plenty of milk. The shells should be intact, without cracks, and the eyes dry and free from mould. Do not buy to store for long periods unless you plan to remove the meat and dry it or freeze it, as coconuts are perishable and usually available all the year round.

To open the coconut The coconut can simply be cracked on a stone or with a hammer, but loss of the water is likely. Try pounding holes in the eyes with a large nail or screwdriver and pouring the water out. The flesh can be removed directly with a knife, but this is facilitated by drying the coconut whole or in large pieces in a 400°F, 200°C oven for 10-15 minutes or placing it over a hot hearth. While still hot, the coconut can then be cracked open and the flesh removed more easily from the shell in large pieces. The flesh can be dried or roasted either in large pieces or after grating, by frying gently or baking at 300°F, 150°C. Constant turning and care is needed to assure even browning. There is an 'old wives' tale' that a child who drinks the coconut water will be a dullard.

To prepare coconut milk The brown layer outside the white coconut meat may or may not be removed before the coconut meat is grated finely on a grater, in a blender being cut into small pieces with a knife, or on a traditional raspado. Pour one cup of boiling water over the coconut meat. Let it stand for thirty minutes. Strain it through a fine sieve. Pour another cup of boiling water over the grated meat and let it stand another thirty minutes. Strain again. The milk collected from the two strainings can be used with the coconut water as a beverage, preferably chilled, or in cooking.

Egusi: *Citrullus colocynthis* (Common name: melon seed Yoruba: *egusi*, Ibo: *ogili*; Hausa: *agusi*) The fruit of this plant can be eaten raw like cucumber or cooked in soups like marrow (summer squash) but in Nigeria it is mainly harvested for its seeds. The black outer shell of the seed is removed manually and the creamy-white inner seed is ground raw or roasted for use in many dishes. In some places, the whole seed is fermented after being soaked in water, boiled and dried and made into a strong substance called ogiri used in preparing soups.

If cooking oil is extracted from the seeds, the residue is also used as food (see Egbalo, Chapter 3). Egusi seeds are high in protein and oil and contain fair amounts of minerals.

To buy Seeds should be selected carefully to be free from discolouration and mould. They should have a pleasant nutty flavour. Egusi seeds can be ground on a stone with a little water just before use, or ground dry for storage. If they are to be stored, grind in a mortar or a coffee grinder until fine but not pasty. The seeds may be roasted or fried (popped) before grinding, depending on taste. Egusi is best stored in the refrigerator after grinding, although if ground when well dried it may be stored in airtight containers at room temperature for some days. Unground dry or roasted seeds may be stored at room temperature for longer periods. Unshelled seeds are even less perishable.

Groundnuts: *Arachis hypogaea* (Common name: peanuts; Yoruba: *epa*; Hausa: *gya'da*; Ibo: *okpa*) Groundnuts are used raw or roasted. When added to stews, they are usually ground and provide flavour and thickening. The quality of protein in groundnuts is more like that of animal protein than most plant foods. It is, however, low in some essential amino-acids and should be supplemented with at least a small amount of meat or fish. Groundnuts also contain a small amount of carbohydrate, many vitamins and minerals and fifty per cent oil, which is primarily unsaturated.

To buy Fresh groundnuts should always be used straight away as sub-optimal storage may result in the production of toxic products by moulds. Groundnuts are sold raw, roasted, shelled or unshelled. Shelled groundnuts may or may not have had the red papery skin removed. *Always* store in a cool dry place. For long storage periods, refrigerate or freeze.

Locust Bean, fermented: *Parkia filicoidae, Parkia biglobosa* (Yoruba: *oru*; Ibo: *eginili-igala*; Efik: *ete-edi-uku*; Hausa: *kalwa*) The fruit of the African locust bean tree has a pulp in which is embedded many small seeds. The pulp is dried in some areas for addition to soups, rice and cereals. A drink called bolola is made from it.

The seeds are used extensively throughout Nigeria as a flavourful and nutritious addition to soups and stews. They contain about 54 per cent fat and 30 per cent protein of high quality, in addition to vitamins and minerals. The seeds are prepared by boiling for twenty-four hours to soften the coats, then pounded and washed several times to remove the broken shells. The kernels are boiled to form a paste which is then fermented, resulting in a very strong-smelling greyish product. This is sold in the markets fresh by the spoonful or in flat dried patties, black in colour.

Oil bean seeds: *Pentaclethra* (Common name: African oil bean; Ibo: *agiri*)   In the eastern part of Nigeria, particularly, the seeds of the African oil bean are commonly fermented and slivered for addition to pottages and stews to which they add texture, protein and oil. Other foods prepared in a similar way and used as a substitute for oil bean include egusi fruits and ukpo seeds. The processed oil beans or substitutes can be purchased from Ibo food traders seasonally in the market.

Sesame seeds   (Benne-seed) Nigeria is one of the largest world producers of benne-seed. It is, however, seldom seen in markets outside of the central regions where it is grown. In these areas it is consumed in large quantities, just as egusi seeds are used elsewhere, and it can be substituted for them in these recipes. Its nutritional value is similar to egusi. Benne-seed can also be used in breads and sweets.

3

The staple foods

We include here foods which provide bulk in the diet. While some of these foods provide valuable vitamins, minerals and some protein, they are mainly carbohydrates, and are usually served with a protein-rich food. Many dishes combining these staple foods with a protein food are described elsewhere in this book.

Acha
Cassava
Cocoyam
Cowpeas ('beans')
Guinea corn and millet
Maize

Plantain and banana
Rice
Sweet potato
Wateryam
Wheat
Yam

Acha

Digitaria exilis. Acha grass is grown for food and straw. In Nigeria, acha grain forms the staple cereal food of the hill tribes of the Jos and Bauchi areas. It is used as a porridge and served as rice with stews. Acha is slightly inferior in protein quality to other cereals common in Nigeria.

Cassava

Manihot utilissima. Common names: manioc, tapioca root, Brazilian arrowroot; Yoruba: *ege* or *gbaguda*; Ibo: *akpu*; Hausa: *rogo*.

Cassava is believed to have been introduced into West Africa from Brazil by Portuguese explorers. It is now one of the most widely cultivated staple foods. It is easy to cultivate, requiring little care and, when processed, can be stored relatively easily. The leaves are used mainly in animal foods, but only the roots are used widely for human consumption. Although the roots of some species are eaten peeled and boiled, cyanide is present in significant amounts in other species. This toxic substance is eliminated by natural fermentation processes in the production of garri and fufu, the most popular products of cassava in Nigeria.

Cassava is a cheap source of carbohydrate, but has little other nutritive value. It should, therefore, always be eaten with protein and vitamin-rich foods.

Preparation of Garri   While garri is usually purchased ready for use, it can be prepared at home, particularly if a special quality is desired. A brief description is given here but, to make your own, it would be best initially to work with someone experienced. The roots are dug up and peeled, usually on the spot. They are then washed and soaked in water for a few hours. Next the roots are grated, packed in a tightly woven but porous bag and weights are placed on the bag for three days to eliminate much of the water. On the fourth day, the bag is opened and the contents spread to dry in the sun for several hours. The grated cassava is then sieved and roasted a little at a time in a pot over a fire. A few drops of palm oil may be added to facilitate roasting and to give colour and flavour. The taste, colour and consistency of garri made in different areas varies. Some garri is preferred for 'drinking' (soaked garri); other types for eba.

Eba (Cooked Garri)   Boil water twice the quantity of the dry garri. Pour the garri on the boiling water quickly, but not all at once. It should be wet throughout the settled mass of grains. Pour off excess water, if any. Mix well with a wooden spoon or the back of a metal one, pressing out any lumps that may have formed. Turn while cooking for two more minutes to ensure that the starch in the garri is well cooked for easy digestion. The consistency should be thick but not too stiff, as it will continue to thicken when cooling. The final product should be stiff enough to form a ball with wet fingers, but not so stiff as to be indigestible. There is a wide range within which personal preference will determine 'digestibility'.

The food value of eba can be improved by using fish, meat or chicken stock instead of water. Eba can be served simply scooped into a bowl, smoothing the surface with the back of a spoon, but it is often moulded quickly in a bowl rinsed with cold water before being turned on to a serving plate. This is one of many thickened carbohydrate foods which are best eaten with fingers after being dipped in stew.

Soaked Garri   Use finely sieved high quality clean garri. Add sufficient cold water to cover. Serve with a little sugar if desired. This is not usually eaten on its own but with roasted groundnuts, fresh coconut, dry fish, fried meat, fried fish or dried meat.

Imoyo Eba

Indigenes of Lagos serve Imoyo Eba with stews. It can be served with any soup or stew and adds considerably to the food value of the garri.

Ingredients	Handy Measure	Metric
Garri, finely sifted	1 mgt	150 g
Margarine or best grade palm oil	2 dsp	20 g
Fish or shrimp stock	$1\frac{1}{2}$ mgt	435 ml
Salt	$\frac{1}{2}$ tsp	1.5 g

Boil the stock, margarine or oil and salt. Pour in the garri little by little, stirring constantly. Cook for 2 minutes turning constantly. The consistency should be firm to the touch and not sticky or too soft.

Preparation of Cassava Fufu   Method 1   Peel and soak the whole cassava in a clay pot for 4-5 days. Grate, sieve and allow to settle. Pound the starch residue (raw cassava paste) in a mortar for five minutes to bind. Place in boiling water in fist-sized balls. The balls should cook for five minutes without breaking up in the water. Remove and pound for 3-4 minutes. Drop the pounded cooked cassava balls into the same water again and boil for another ten minutes. Remove and pound until the cassava fufu leaves the sides of the mortar and forms a lump. Eat as other thickened carbohydrate foods.

Preparation of Cassava Fufu   Method II   Soak the whole cassava tubers, which have been peeled, in water for 4-5 days. They will now be soft. Remove the central hard core and cook the outer part. Pound.

Preparation of Cassava Fufu   Method III   Soak the whole cassava tubers, which have been peeled, in water for 4-5 days. They will now be soft. Remove the central hard core and dry the outer part. Add hot water when pounding.

Preparation of Cassava for Edible Starch   Newly harvested cassava tubers are peeled, washed in water and crushed in a machine or grated. The pulped cassava is then squeezed through a woven raffia bag or a tightly woven porous cloth bag. The liquid squeezed out is allowed to stand until the starch settles. The water is poured off and the starch cooked for food.

Farina The crude grated cassava residue remaining in the preparation of starch is used as a snack food and in making some desserts.

Cooking of Cassava Starch

Ingredients	Handy Measure	Metric
Wet starch	1 tpt	60 g
Palm oil	½ tsp	1.5 ml
Water	2 tpt	140 ml

Starch as sold in the market is usually in solid chunks which are not completely dry. If dry starch is used, more water will be required. Dissolve the starch in water. Rub oil over the bottom of a thick skillet. Pour in the starch and water mixture and turn on the heat. Stir constantly with a wooden spoon until the starch forms a soft mass. The mass will be opaque at first, but with continued cooking and pressing, it will become partly translucent. Cool slightly before eating. Use a wet finger and thumb to 'cut' the starch into bite-sized portions which are then dipped into the accompanying soup or stew.

Thickened Dried Cassava and Maize

Idah: *Oja-Pa*

Ingredients	Handy Measure	Metric
Grated dry cassava	1 mt	100 g
Ground dry maize	2 mt	125 g
Water	3 mt or more	570 ml or more

Use ground dry cassava (lafu) purchased in the market. This is not garri as the cassava is not soaked to prepare it. Mix the cassava, maize and water in a pot. Cook, stirring constantly with a wooden spoon until well thickened. Continue for a few minutes more when it will draw away from the sides of the pot. Cool partially and serve with okro soup or a leafy green vegetable soup. (Dried cassava and maize already combined are sold in some markets; prepare with water as above.)

Cocoyam

There are several varieties of cocoyam. The main ones are *Xanthosoma sagittifolium* (Tannia) believed to be from the West Indies, and *Colocasia esculentum* (Taro) introduced from India. *Xanthosoma* leaves are bright green with separate lobes, whereas *Colocasia* leaves are paler green with the lobes closed at the base. Both types grow to about 180 centimetres in height and have very large leaves. The young leaves are sometimes eaten but the main source of food is the underground stem or corm. In many areas of Nigeria, cocoyam is considered to be an inferior food to other yams. Nutritionally, however, it is similar and could provide valuable variation to the diet. Cocoyam contains a good quantity of carbohydrate and some vitamins, minerals and incomplete protein. Both the root and the leaves of the cocoyam must be cooked well. If not, the oxalates present in it are most irritating to the throat.

Boiled Cocoyam Cut the cocoyam into large pieces or leave it whole. Cocoyam may be peeled or left unpeeled. If unpeeled, wash thoroughly before cooking. Cook in boiling water to which salt and pepper have been added to taste. When easily pierced with a fork, drain and serve. Unpeeled cocoyam may be peeled before serving or when eating.

Roasted Cocoyam Wash the cocoyam well. Large cocoyam may be cut into pieces; small ones can be roasted whole. Place on glowing charcoal or embers of fire-wood. When easily pierced with a fork, remove and peel. Serve with superior palm oil, fish oil, or simple stew. Serve with Prepared Pepper or Smoked Fish 'Butter'. Cocoyam may also be baked in the oven at 350°F, 180°C, although the smoked flavour will not be present.

Steamed Grated Cocoyam Wash the cocoyam and grate it, using the grater you use for coconut or even a slightly coarser one. If desired, you can add salt to taste and a teaspoon of oil to 450g of cocoyam for colour. Cut banana leaves into squares after removing the midrib. Wrap spoonfuls of cocoyam in long rectangular moulds of lightly oiled banana leaves (see illustration). Steam as for Steamed Cowpea Paste for thirty minutes. Cool slightly before unwrapping so that the moulded cocoyam is easily removed. Serve with leafy green vegetable stews.

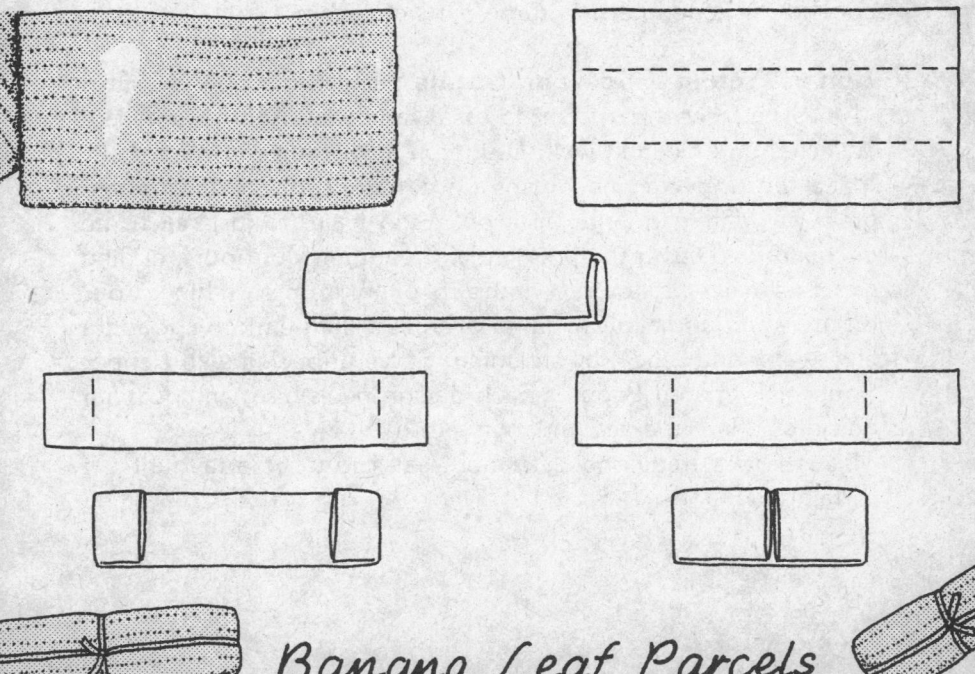

Banana Leaf Parcels

Mashed Cocoyam and Palm Oil

Ingredients	Handy Measure	Metric
Cocoyam	2 medium	250 g
Palm oil	½ mt	85 ml
Dry fish, flaked	1 mgt	230 g
Onion, chopped	1 mt	190 g
Salt and dry red pepper	to taste	

Scrub and bake or boil the cocoyam in its jacket. Peel and mash. Add salt, pepper, palm oil, flaked dry fish and chopped onion. Place on the fire and stir for 10 minutes, turning to prevent burning.
This could be served with a salad or cooked vegetable as a complete meal.

Fried Cocoyam Peel and slice the cocoyam into pieces half a centimetre thick. Fry in hot fat until light brown. Serve immediately with any meat or fish stew or with simple palm oil or groundnut oil stew.

Pounded Cocoyam Boil the peeled cocoyam in unsalted water until tender. Pound in a mortar, adding water in small amounts until it forms a mass. Some varieties do not easily form a mass. These are often pounded with garri. Use about one part cooked thickened garri to three parts cocoyam.

Boiled Young Cocoyam Corms The very young, small (10-15 cm) secondary corms of a variety of *Xanthosoma* are collected and cleaned well. Dry them in the sun for three days. Place the unpeeled cocoyams on a thick support of elephant grass or raffia in a large thick pot. Add water to just reach the cocoyam and cover the pot tightly. Steam for four hours, adding water as necessary to prevent the cocoyam from scorching. Pour off the water and allow to stand overnight. In the morning, add a little water and reheat by steaming. Serve unpeeled with Pepper Soup or Prepared Pepper. Each person peels his own cocoyam and dips it into the accompanying dish.
This is a very traditional seasonal treat said to be a favourite of certain Ijaw Gods.

Cowpeas

Vigna unguiculate (Common name: beans; black-eyed peas). Many legumes are used in cooking throughout Nigeria. While the pods of most of them can be eaten when fresh and young as a green vegetable, the vast majority of 'beans and peas' are dried. The most widespread and readily available 'bean' is the cowpea, of which there are numerous varieties. All varieties are similar in food value, but local preferences exist. In cooking, the colour imparted to foods and the amount of water and time required in cooking varies from one type to another. Cowpeas are high in protein and soluble carbohydrate, low in oil and contain some minerals. The quality of the protein is good but incomplete, so it should be supplemented with some animal protein. In Nigeria, where animal protein is in short supply and the diet is predominantly carbohydrate, cowpeas are a most valuable source of protein.

To Buy and Store Select cowpeas that are well dried, free of discolouration and of insects and insect holes. Before use, they should be picked over to remove debris, foreign materials and damaged peas. It may be necessary, if the cowpeas are of poor quality, to wash them several times in cold water, pouring off the floating debris with each rinse. They should then be dried well in the sun or in an oven at 225°F, 110°C.

If buying cowpeas in bulk it is difficult to keep them from becoming infested with weavils. An effective, simple means of preserving them is to shake the clean, dry cowpeas in a small amount of groundnut oil (5 mg oil to 1 kg cowpeas) to coat them thinly. This method has been found to protect the cowpeas for up to eight months.

Cowpeas are cooked in two forms: whole or as a processed paste. Recipes using whole beans as the main ingredient are given first. Other recipes using cowpeas as a secondary ingredient can be located in the index. Secondly the preparation of cowpea paste is given, followed by recipes utilising it. An excellent book for those interested in more details about cowpeas and their preparation can be found in the Reading List at the end of this book.

Boiled Cowpeas

Ingredients	Handy Measure	Metric
Clean cowpeas	1 mgt	230 g
Water	2 mgt	280 ml
Salt	1 tsp	3 g

The cowpeas may be boiled directly or soaked for a few hours before boiling to save fuel and time. Bring the cowpeas, water and salt to the boil, lower the heat and simmer until the water is absorbed and the beans are soft but not mushy. (It may be necessary to add more water towards the end of the cooking time). Cooking can take between 30 minutes and 1 hour, depending on the variety of cowpeas and how dry they are.
Serve boiled cowpeas with boiled rice and a simple meat or fish stew.

Cowpea and Plantain Pottage

Ingredients	Handy Measure	Metric
Clean cowpeas	1 mgt	230 g
Firm, ripe plantain*	1/2 large	200 g
Palm oil, best quality	1 tpt	70 ml
Dry fish, cleaned	1 small	120 g
Onion	1 small	75 g
Fresh pepper	3 ata rodo	20 g
Salt	to taste	
Water	3 mgt	870 ml

*Yam, sweet potato or vegetable marrow (summer squash) could be used instead of plantain.

Grind the onion and fresh pepper. Boil the cowpeas in plenty of water until soft (about 1 hour). Drain the cowpeas and then add 1 mgt water. Cut the plantain into 1 cm cubes and cover with water. Cook for 5-10 minutes, until easily pierced with a fork. Add the cowpeas and remaining ingredients and cook for another 20 minutes. The cowpeas and plantain should still be recognisable, although very soft. Serve with eko or garri.

Soft Boiled Cowpeas
Yoruba: *Awuje*

Ingredients	Handy Measure	Metric
Clean cowpeas	1 mgt	230 g
Potash or	small pinch	
Salt	½ tsp	1.5 g
Water		

Cover the cowpeas with water and bring to the boil. Pour off water. Cover beans again with water, bring to the boil and pour off the water. Add 2 mgt cold water and potash or salt; bring to the boil. Lower the heat and cook slowly until the water has been absorbed and the cowpeas are very soft. Add a little more water near the end of cooking if necessary, but the cowpeas should be very thick and mushy.
Serve with eko, bread and palm oil or groundnut stew. When hawked on the street, awuje is served with mussel shells rather than spoons.

Cowpea Stew
Yoruba: *Gbegiri*

Ingredients	Handy Measure	Metric
Cowpeas	1 mgt	230 g
Okro, grated (optional)	6 medium	240 g
Dry ground red pepper	1 tsp	2 g
Onion, ground	1 small	75 g
Dry crayfish	1 tpt	40 g
Fresh tomato, ground	1 large	120 g
Salt	to taste	
Water	2 mgt	580 ml
Potash, ground	½ tsp	1.5 g

Soak the cowpeas and remove their skins (see page 41). Bring to the boil with potash in 2 mgt of water, turn down the heat and cook until soft. Mash or sieve the beans. Add pepper, onion, tomato and salt and cook for twenty minutes on a low heat, stirring frequently to prevent scorching. Add dry crayfish and okro and cook for 2-3 minutes. Serve with amala, eba or eko.

Frejon
Cowpea and Coconut Dish

This is a Brazilian dish brought to Lagos in the last century. It is especially well known to Catholics, who eat it on Good Friday.

Ingredients	Handy Measure	Metric
Clean cowpeas (dark brown variety preferred)	1 mgt	230 g
Coconut	1 large	1100 g
Water	3 mgt	1 l
Cloves	3-4	
Sugar	to taste	
Salt	to taste	

Boil the cowpeas in water until mushy, using a low heat to avoid scorching. Mash into a smooth paste with a wooden spoon and sieve to a purée (or use an electric blender). Prepare the coconut milk (see Chapter 2). Add coconut milk and cloves to the cowpeas. Boil uncovered until very thick, stirring frequently (about $1\frac{1}{2}$ hours). Add a little sugar and a very little salt to taste.
The consistency should be like thick cream. It is served with fish stew and dry 'garri aguda' (farina). It could also be served as a dessert, in small quantities, garnished with cream.

Frejon with Meat
Common name: puréed cowpeas with meat; Yoruba: *rejoada*

Ingredients	Handy Measure	Metric
Cowpeas (dark brown type preferred)	1 mgt	230 g
Coconut	1 large	1100 g
Onion	1 small	75 g
Tomato (fresh)	2 small	150 g
Fresh pepper	2 ata rodo or	6 g
	1 tatasai	35 g
Tongue, pork and tripe	1 mgt	225 g

Prepare the coconut milk (see Chapter 2).

Boil the beans and tongue, pork and tripe (to prepare tripe, see Chapter 4), until the beans are very soft and the meats are tender. Remove the meats and put aside. Add the tomato, onion and pepper to the beans and purée in a blender or press through a sieve. Season and add the coconut milk. Cook on low heat for 30 minutes uncovered until thickened. Add cooked meats and serve.

Serve with eba, fine garri (farina) or boiled yam or rice. Well-seasoned Frejon with Meat can be thinned and served as an appetizer soup.

Cowpea Paste

Cowpea paste is simply hulled cowpeas which have been ground to a smooth consistency. The preparation of cowpea paste is not simple, but it is important to learn to do it well as it is the basic ingredient of many delicious and nutritious steamed and fried dishes.

Cowpea paste can be prepared in quantity and frozen in convenient sized packets, but the flavour is better if the beans are hulled, frozen and then ground just before use.

To Hull the Cleaned Cowpeas Soak the cowpeas in plenty of water for ten minutes (longer soaking does not make hulling any easier and in some varieties actually makes it more difficult). Drain the water, rub handfuls of the beans firmly between the palms of the hands several times in quick succession. Fill the bowl with water, mix with the beans and pour off the floating hulls. Repeat the rubbing and draining process several times until most of the cowpeas are hulled. This may take about five minutes with two mgt of cowpeas. Any remaining husked cowpeas can be hulled individually; any husks left on the cowpeas will lower the quality of the paste. If the cowpea paste is to be used in a fried dish, the cowpeas should be drained and ground at this point to minimize the amount of water necessary for grinding. If the paste is to be used in a steamed dish, the cowpeas can be soaked in water until needed, several hours if need be.

Alternatively, the soaked cowpeas can be given a 1-2 second spin in a blender to remove the hulls, which are then separated in the manual method described previously.

To Grind Hulled Cowpeas The cowpeas can be ground on a stone, in a mortar, or in any mechanical grinder or blender which can provide a smooth product without the addition of an excessive amount of water. If they are to be ground on a stone or in a mortar a little water may need to be added. If they are to be ground in a blender, the amount of water to be added will depend on the power of the motor. The important thing is to add as little water as possible, so that when other ingredients are added the paste does not become too watery. As a guide, however, a mt of dry beans will yield two mt of soaked hulled cowpeas. Two mt of soaked, hulled cowpeas will take approximately two mt of water to grind in an average sized blender. This paste will not need any water added for most recipes.

To Whip the Paste Almost all the recipes using cowpea paste require the incorporation of air into the paste to give the final product a soufflé-like quality. This is not possible in a blender or on a stone. Thus, after the cowpeas have been ground, they must be whipped, either with a mortar, a wire whisk or a hand or electric mixer. The paste should be whipped well. As a guide, five minutes or more whipping is needed for paste produced from two mgt beans, except when using an electric mixer. Adhering seed coats will prevent the paste from being light, as will the addition of other ingredients such as tomato and onion. If these ingredients are added, they should be mixed in quickly just before cooking.

Cowpea Paste Prepared From Cowpea Flour Cowpea flour is sold commercially or can be prepared in the home. The

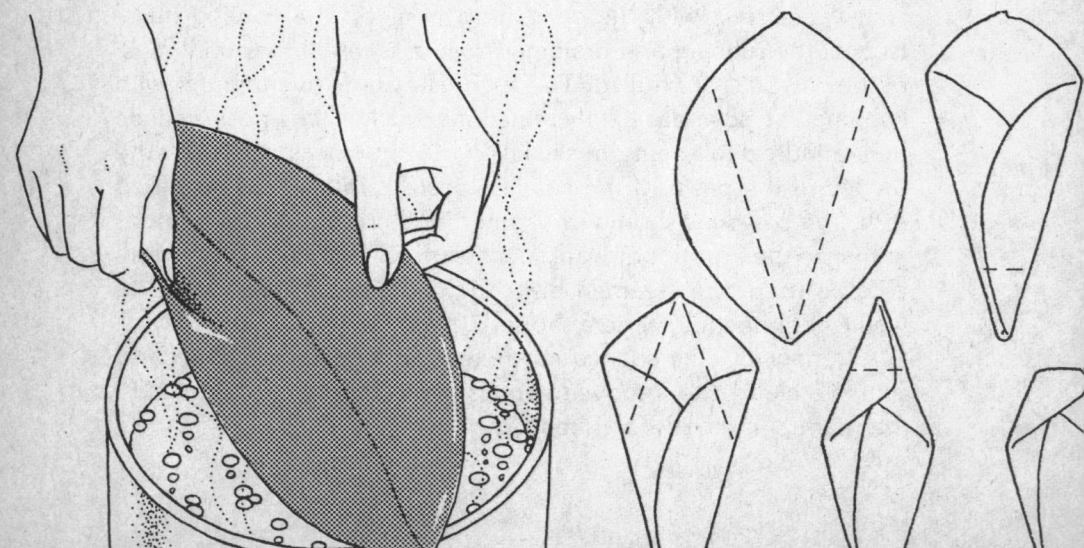

cowpeas are hulled and then dried before being ground in a flour mill (manual or engine powered). This flour is then mixed with water and whipped to a consistency like that of the freshly-prepared paste.

Steamed Dishes Prepared with Cowpea Paste Steamed cowpea paste foods are similar in preparation and consistency, but finer in texture than the savoury steamed puddings of Europe.

Steamed foods prepared with cowpea paste are traditionally wrapped in leaves (*Thaumatococcus sp.* or *Sarcophrynium sp.*) before cooking. The leaves used are usually available in the local markets, but they are becoming increasingly expensive. Cut banana or plantain leaves tied with raffia or string can also be used, though the product will have a different shape. Whichever leaves are used, they should be held over boiling water briefly to wilt them so they will fold without cracking. Leaves give a special flavour to wrapped steamed foods but, if they are unavailable, squares of greaseproof (parchment) paper can be used; tinfoil is not good as steam does not reach the food. Oiled tins, e.g. milk tins or other moulds can also be used. These should be filled three-quarters full and covered loosely with tinfoil or have waxed or greaseproof paper tied over the top. The prepared packages are placed in a steamer, like the one below. A commercial steamer with a metal support or basket can be used, or an improvised one can be just as effective. Use sticks or leaves to form a support on which to rest the packages. Pour water half way up the support. It is important that water should not reach the packages, even when boiling, because they are to be cooked by

Cowpea Paste Parcels

steam. Cover the pot with a tight lid and cook for the recommended time. Take out one package and test to see if it is done; return to the fire if it is not well set. Add more water to the pot if necessary during cooking. When cooked, the food should be firm, but not hard, with no 'beany' taste or smell. Cooking time will vary depending on the size of the packages and the quantity of them. It will probably take over an hour. You can use a pressure cooker, following the manufacturer's instructions for steamed puddings. Serve wrapped or unwrapped. The packages will not unwrap cleanly when hot. If they are to be kept for more than a few hours, refrigerate or store them over the hearth. Then reheat, if desired, in a steamer or in the oven.

Simple Steamed Cowpea Paste (Yoruba: *ekuru*) Cowpea paste prepared as described above is whipped until very light, with hot water added gradually to make a thin, but not watery, consistency. Wrap in leaves or place in moulds and steam. When cool, serve crumbled in large chunks mixed with a simple palm oil stew. Serve as a lunch or supper dish, with boiled yam, eko or bread.

Moyin-moyin
Seasoned Steamed Cowpea Paste

Ingredients	Handy Measure	Metric
Cowpea paste	1 mgt	225 g
Ground onion, chopped finely	2 dsp	18 g
Dry, ground red pepper	1 tsp	2 g
Good palm oil	4 dsp	28 ml
Salt	1½ tsp	4.5 g

Prepare cowpea paste as described previously. Stir in the oil which has been warmed, then blend in other ground ingredients as desired (suggestions on page 45). Add hot water slowly until the mixture coats the back of a spoon: a thick running consistency. Add salt to taste. Fold in any chunky ingredients as desired (suggestions on page 45). Wrap in leaves or put in moulds, three-quarters full. Steam, tightly covered, for 60 minutes.
Moyin-moyin is traditionally served with ogi, eko, or soaked garri. It also goes well with rice dishes and salads. It can be cut into

small bite-sized pieces for cocktail snacks.
Additions to be blended in   A beaten whole egg; ground fresh pepper instead of dry pepper (quantity to taste); 2 dsp tomato paste; ½ tpt ground dry crayfish; pinch of dry ginger or one tsp chopped fresh ginger; groundnut oil instead of palm oil.
Additions to be folded in   Fold in one or more of the following just before moulding: ½ tpt fish, flaked or in small chunks; 1 tpt fresh crayfish, cut into pieces; ½ tpt corned beef, crumbled; 1 boiled egg, quartered; ½ tpt chopped ham, bacon or liver (boiled).

Steamed Cowpea Paste with Egusi: I
Yoruba: *Igbalo*

Ingredients	Handy Measure	Metric
Cowpea paste	1 mgt	230 g
Egusi seeds*, ground	½ mgt	100 g
Dry red pepper	1 tsp	2 g
Potash	small pinch	
Salt	to taste	

*the residue left after extracting egusi seed oil can also be used.

Prepare the cowpea paste as described previously. Grind the egusi until smooth. Mix the cowpea paste, egusi, potash (softened in a tsp. warm water) and salt to taste. Whip, adding the hot water gradually until the mixture coats the back of a spoon thickly. Mould, steam and cool as previously described. Serve with a simple palm oil stew and eko, ogi, bread or rice. This is also nice with a salad for a light lunch.
Variations   Egusi seeds may be used roasted or unroasted. You may add 2 dsp. onion and 1 fresh pepper, and/or 3 dsp. fresh tomato, chopped or ground and fried before adding; ½ tpt dry ground crayfish; ½ tsp. whole dry crayfish (heads and tails removed).

Steamed Cowpea Paste with Egusi: II
Yoruba: *Jogi*

Prepare as for Steamed Cowpea Paste I above, but use a greater proportion of egusi (e.g. 1 mgt egusi and ½ mgt cowpea paste). This is similar in consistency to an omelette and very nutritious.

Light Akara
Fried Cowpea Paste Fritters

In many parts of the country, akara is sold, in the morning and the evening, directly out of the oil. This is very convenient for workers, school children and for people needing light meals!

Ingredients	Handy Measure	Metric
Cowpea paste	1 mgt	230 g
Chopped onion	2 dsp	18 g
Dry ground red pepper	$\frac{1}{2}$ tsp	1 g
Salt	$\frac{1}{2}$ tsp	1.5 g
Palm oil or groundnut oil for deep frying		

The cowpea paste should be whipped very well to incorporate air. Warm water is added slowly until a thick dropping consistency is obtained. If the batter scatters when dropped in the oil, it is too watery. Fold any other ingredients desired (onion, salt, pepper) into the whipped paste just before cooking; repeat with each batch of akara to be fried. This will ensure that the whipped batter loses the minimum of air and that the water and paste do not separate. Heat the oil until it just begins to smoke. Drop the batter by dessertspoonfuls (or larger spoons if desired) into the hot fat. When they are brown on the underside, flip them over and allow them to brown on the other side. Before removing them from the oil, press to squeeze out the excess oil. This is not always necessary, depending on the consistency of the batter and the desired appearance of the final product.

Light akara is best served immediately it is cooked. If it must be stored, refry or heat in a hot oven. Akara is eaten with ogi, eko, or bread for breakfast, or as a snack.

Variations Mix one egg into the batter when whipping; add coarsely chopped whole dry pepper; add coarsely chopped whole fresh pepper; and 2 okro, chopped finely.

Heavy Akara
Ijesha style

Ijesha akara is similar to light akara, except that very little water is used to prepare the paste and none is added to it before frying. It does not need to be whipped. Use a round calabash or round soup ladle to scoop the batter into the hot oil. The resulting product will be spherical, very solid and heavy. This type of akara is a nutritious and substantial meal in itself. It is eaten as light akara. It can be flavoured with ground or whole dry crayfish or with dry fish broken into small pieces.

Cowpea Dumplings
Dan wake

Ingredients	Handy Measure	Metric
Cowpea flour	1½ mgt	270 g
Potash, crushed	1 tsp.	3 g
Water	1 mgt (approx)	200 ml
Salt	1 tsp.	3 g

Dissolve the potash in water and mix in the cowpea flour. Let it stand for 15-20 minutes. Add salt to taste. The mixture should be of a thick dropping consistency. Fill a large cooking pot two-thirds full with water and bring to the boil. Drop dessertspoonfuls of cowpea mixture into the rapidly boiling water and cook for 3-5 minutes. Drain and rinse twice. Serve as a meal garnished with dry red pepper and sesame or egusi oil.
Variations Dried herbs may be mixed into the batter for additional flavour and colour. Drop small spoonfuls into meat or fish broth for an appetizer soup.

Guinea Corn (Sorghum) and Millet

Sorghum and millet are grown mainly in those areas of Nigeria with dry climates. They are nutritionally similar to maize (corn) in protein and carbohydrate, but low in minerals and vitamins. Both are cooked in similar ways and can be used interchangeably. They are also used to prepare a variety of alcoholic beverages.

To Buy Select guinea corn and millet in the market carefully. It should look clean and bright, and lack insect holes and insects. Clean the grains well before using. They will need to be picked over carefully to remove foreign matter, sand and husks. Flour can be prepared from the well-cleaned and dried product in manual or electric mills in the market. It should be milled at least twice to obtain a fine texture. Try using this flour as a substitute for part (up to a third) of the wheat flour in bread or biscuit recipes. You may need to add more liquid than allowed for in the recipe.

Thickened Ground Millet or Guinea Corn
Tuwo dawa

A whole grain porridge or thickened carbohydrate food.

Ingredients	Handy Measure	Metric
Guinea corn or millet	1 mgt	150 g
Water for porridge	$2\frac{1}{2}$ mgt	725 ml
Water for serving with stew	$1\text{-}1\frac{1}{2}$ mgt	290-435 ml

The guinea corn or millet may be ground according to taste and use. As a porridge, it may be preferred coarsely ground and cooked with sufficient water to result in a product like ogi or oat porridge. As an accompaniment to stew, a fine flour may be preferred with little water, resulting in a thickened carbohydrate food more like eba or eko.

Mix the ground grain and water. Bring to a boil, stirring constantly to prevent lumps. Continue to cook turning well for 2 minutes after it thickens. Serve as a cereal with milk and sugar to taste. Serve as a thickened carbohydrate, partially cooled (it will thicken further with cooling) with kuku soup or a leafy green stew.

Millet Balls
Hausa: *Fura Gero*

Ingredients	Handy Measure	Metric
Millet	2 mt	250 g
Ground rice	$\frac{1}{2}$ mt	65 g
Dry ground red pepper	1 tsp	2 g
Sugar	to taste	
Spice (African nutmeg, cinnamon)	$\frac{1}{2}$ tsp	1 g

Prepare flour from the millet. Add ground spice and pepper. Bind with a little cold water, making a very stiff dough. Shape into small balls and drop into boiling water. Boil for 10 minutes. Drain and beat balls in a mortar. Re-form and toss in ground rice flour. Serve with sugar and fresh milk or yoghurt for breakfast.

Hot Cooked Fermented Millet Flour
Ogi baba

Use cleaned guinea corn or millet and prepare in the same way as maize for Ogi. *Ogi baba* is usually served for breakfast or before bed. Some people like it watered down as a drink. Sugar or milk may be added before serving. The length of time the guinea corn or millet is soaked before processing determines the degree of 'sourness'. Igalla people sometimes grind a pod of enge with 5 congos of grain. The delicate colour and scent of this product is most appealing.

Maize

Maize is the most important cereal crop grown in the southern parts of Nigeria, but is popular throughout the country. It is eaten fresh, roasted or boiled, and the dried kernels are ground or fermented for various foods.

While maize proteins are of a relatively poor quality, improved varieties are being introduced. Maize is a good source of carbohydrate, but should always be served with some good quality protein.

Boiled Maize   The maize raised for food in Nigeria is shared by man and his animals. It is the hard variety that dries and stores relatively well. If it is to be boiled, it is best picked when young and early in the day, just before cooking because then the corn is very tender and sweet. Most Nigerians also enjoy it when it is quite firm and less sweet. The corn may be husked or partly husked. It is then dropped into boiling salted water and covered until it is easily pierced with a fork (20 minutes to 1 hour, depending on its maturity). Boiled corn is served as a snack, often with fresh coconut.

Boiled Dry Maize Wash and clean the dry maize well and add to boiling water. Add salt ($\frac{1}{2}$ tsp. to 1 mgt). Cook for $1\frac{1}{2}$ hours or more until very soft, adding water as necessary. This can be eaten with coconut or served with butter, shea butter, black oil or the best grade palm oil. Traditionally, shea butter (Yoruba: *ori*, extracted from seeds of the Emi tree) and black grease (extracted from palm kernel) were eaten with boiled dry maize. Both fats can be found in local markets with difficulty.

Roasted Maize in the Husk Remove only the outermost leaves from the maize. Immerse each ear in water, remove and then place over a wood or charcoal fire. Turn and when well browned (30 minutes or more), husk and eat.

Husked Roasted Maize Husk the maize and roast directly over charcoal or wood embers, browning on all sides. Eat as a snack with fresh coconut.

Fermented Corn Starch Clean dry maize kernels, picking them over carefully. Soak them in water overnight or up to two days, depending on taste. Drain the maize and grind in a mill (hand or machine) in the market. Sieve ground maize several times in a very fine sieve, using large amounts of water. Allow the starch to settle in the water, either all day or overnight. Drain and store the fermented cornflour in the refrigerator with some water to cover. It will keep several weeks this way. It will keep even longer if frozen. Remove more water by pouring the starch into a finely woven cloth bag and pressing out as much water as possible. Place in airtight containers or plastic bags in the freezer.

Hot Cooked Fermented Cornstarch
Ogi

Boil 3-4 tpt water (depending on how wet the cornstarch is). Mix 1 tpt fermented cornstarch with 4 dsp. of boiling water in a cooking utensil. Pour the remaining boiling water over the wet starch stirring constantly to prevent lumps forming. Return to the heat for a few minutes to cook the starch thoroughly. Serve hot in bowls with or without sugar and evaporated (thinned) milk. Ogi is often eaten with dodo or akara for breakfast or a light evening meal. Some chocolate-drink granules can be mixed with the boiling water for variety. To increase the food value, especially important for babies and growing children, stir a well beaten egg into the ogi immediately after removing from the fire.

Moulded Cooked Fermented Cornstarch
Eko

Ingredients	Handy Measure	Metric
Wet fermented cornstarch	1 tpt	90 g
Water, depending on how wet the cornstarch is	2-3 tpt	140-210 ml

Boil the water. Mix the cornstarch to a smooth paste with a little cold water. Pour the boiling water over the starch stirring constantly to prevent lumps forming. Boil for a few minutes to cook the starch thoroughly. Wrap in clean leaves as for Steamed Cornflour Paste and cool. Serve in leaves or unmoulded with a variety of foods as suggested throughout this book. In many parts of Nigeria, eko is sold at meal times on the streets and is purchased by workers to eat with moyin-moyin, beans or simple stews.

Ground Maize Steamed Pudding
Ijaw: *Aka ikpa*

Ingredients	Handy Measure	Metric
Finely ground maize	5½ dsp	50 g
Over-ripe plantain	½ medium	120 g
Salt	½ tsp	1.5 g
Dry ground red pepper	1 tsp	2 g
Best quality palm oil	1½ dsp	13 g
Potash	pinch	
Water	½ mgt	145 ml

Clean and grind the maize in a mill to a very fine meal. Mash or pound the over-ripe plantain and mix with the maize. Add the warm oil, potash, salt and pepper, then add the water slowly until it is of a thick pouring consistency. Wrap in leaves and steam as described for cowpea paste dishes.

Cooked Maize Meal

Ingredients	Handy Measure	Metric
Finely ground corn	1 mgt	225 g
Water	3 mgt	870 ml

Boil the water. Add the finely ground dry corn and stir. Cook for 2 minutes to ensure that the starch is well cooked. Pour into a bowl and cool until it becomes firm, with a consistency like eko. Serve with agbono soup, leafy green stews or groundnut stews.

Fresh Maize Steamed in Leaves

Ibo: *Ikpakpala, osu oka*

Ingredients	Handy Measure	Metric
Fresh maize	2 cobs	
Salt	$\frac{1}{2}$ tsp	1.5 g
Onion	$\frac{1}{2}$ small	50 g
Fresh pepper	2 ata rodo or 1 tsp dry ground	
Palm oil	1 dsp	9 ml
Dry crayfish, ground	$\frac{1}{2}$ tpt	15 g

Grind the maize kernels until smooth. Add the remaining ingredients (the onion and fresh pepper should be ground before adding) and mix until smooth. Consistency and subsequent wrapping and steaming should be as for Moyin-moyin.

Plantain and Bananas

Plantain: *Musa sapientum, var. Paradisiaca* (Common name: Cooking banana): Banana: *Musa sapientum* Both plantain and bananas are important sources of carbohydrate for man. In Nigeria, bananas are usually eaten ripe as a fruit. Cooked green plantain is one of the main staple foods in the Delta region of Nigeria. Cooked ripe plantain (dodo) is enjoyed throughout Nigeria, but is becoming increasingly expensive, making it almost a delicacy.

Ripe banana and plantain carbohydrate is mainly in the form of easily digestible sugars; unripe banana and plantain carbohydrate is mainly starch. Both fruits have very little protein but contain valuable amounts of vitamins and minerals. Recipes in this chapter contain only plantain; many other recipes using plantain can be found in the Index.

To Buy Buy green plantain which is plump, with firm, juicy skins, bright green in colour. It will ripen within a few days. If the plantain is to be used immediately, buy fingers which are bright yellow and firm. Do not store plantain in the refrigerator to ripen as the normal ripening processes will not take place.

Roasted Plantain Peeled ripe or mid-ripe plantain is placed in the glowing charcoal or over a grill and turned to cook evenly. When it is easily pierced with a fork, remove it. If it is cooked in the charcoal, scrape it with a knife before eating. Serve as a snack with groundnuts or as part of a simple meal with the best grade of palm oil, roast fish or a simple stew or sauce. Plantain can also be roasted under a broiler, though the flavour is not so good. If the plantain is very thick, cut it in half length-wise before broiling.

Boiled Peeled Plantain Use green or mid-ripe plantain, depending on taste. Scrape the outer surface slightly with a knife if desired, to smooth the surface. Cut into large pieces or leave whole. Boil in water containing salt and dry red pepper. Eat with any soup or stew. This is especially nice with pepper soups and fish stews. Alternatively, serve with the best palm oil and roast fish or meat.

Another method of cooking peeled plantain is to add a pinch of potash and $\frac{1}{2}$ tsp. of salt to 3 green plantain. Cover them with water, put on a lid and cook for ten minutes. Uncover and cook until they are tender and most of the water has evaporated. This method produces a dark red/brown coloured coating on the plantain.

Boiled Ripe Plantain Peel the ripe plantain and cut each finger into 2 or 3 pieces. Just cover the plantain with salted water. Boil until it is easily pierced with a fork (about 10-15 minutes). Serve on its own or with bean stew or a leafy green vegetable stew. Try slicing it into pieces 1 cm thick and boiling it for five minutes, or until tender. Serve with butter or palm oil and salt as a side dish with rice and a meat or fish stew.

Boiled Unpeeled Green Plantain Cut ripe or unripe plantain into equal lengths of about ten cm. Wash and place them in a pot with enough cold water to cover. Cook until soft. Remove the skin and arrange on a serving dish. Sprinkle with dry ground red pepper and serve hot with boiled beans.

Pounded Green Plantain (Ijaw: *obubu fiai*) Cut 1 ripe and 2 unripe plantain (unpeeled) into 2-3 pieces each. Put them into a pot with enough water to cover and cook until soft. Peel and pound unripe plantain. Remove from mortar. Peel and pound ripe plantain and mix with the unripe pounded ones. Then mix and pound adding $\frac{1}{2}$ tsp. salt and 2 dsp. oil to taste. Shape into individual rounded servings or serve as eba. Among the Kolokumas of the Ijaws this food is for the Gods, wealthy people and the newly circumcised.

Boiled Ripe Plantain and Cooked Cassava Starch (*Eguobobo*) Boil the ripe plantain until soft. Prepare cooked cassava starch. Pound the plantain and starch together in a mortar and serve with banga soup. (The proportions of the two foods are determined by taste).

Dodo (Fried Ripe Plantain) The plantain to be used for dodo may be just ripe or even over-ripe, depending on taste. Remove the skin of the plantain. Cut into round or lengthwise thin slices ($\frac{1}{4}$ cm thick) or into large or small chunks, again depending on taste and how they are to be served. As a garnish or side dish, thin round slices or small cubes may be preferred; as a snack, large chunks may be appropriate; as the main food of a light meal with stew, lengthwise slices may be appropriate. Season lightly with salt. Heat the oil (palm oil or vegetable oil) 1 cm deep in a frying pan. Fry the plantain one layer at a time so as not to reduce the heat and to prevent the pieces from sticking to each other. When they are light to medium brown on both sides remove them from the oil and drain. Serve hot. Children love dodo!

Plantain Flour Plantain flour is used traditionally in several ways. It can also be used as a substitute for wheat flour in breads and biscuits (cookies). Substitute $\frac{1}{2}$ tpt in each mgt of wheat flour.

Peel the ripe plantain and slice very thinly. Dry on a clean board or a stainless steel or plastic tray until crisp. Grind in a hand or machine mill or pound in a mortar to produce a fine flour. Green banana flour can be prepared in the same way.

Steamed Plantain Pudding I

Ingredients	Handy Measure	Metric
Unripe plantain flour	5½ dsp	50 g
Ripe plantain	½ medium	120 g
Dry ground red pepper	½ tsp	1 g
Salt	½ tsp	1.5 g
Onion, chopped finely	1½ dsp	15 g
Water (hot)	8 dsp	72 ml
Plantain leaves		

Wash, peel and pound the ripe plantain in a mortar until free from lumps. (A blender can be used, but slice the plantain thinly first). Put into a bowl and add the unripe plantain flour, salt, pepper, onion and water to make a thick dropping consistency. Wrap and steam as for Steamed Cowpea Paste. Serve hot or cold as a snack or with any stew.

Steamed Plantain Pudding II

Ingredients	Handy Measure	Metric
Unripe plantain flour	5½ dsp	50 g
Over-ripe plantain	½ medium	120 g
Salt	½ tsp	1.5 g
Pepper, dry red	½ tsp	1 g
Fresh superior palm oil	2 dsp	6 ml
Potash	pinch	

Soften the potash in a few drops of water. Pound with the over-ripe plantain, salt, pepper and oil. Add plantain flour to give a thick dropping consistency. Wrap and steam as for Steamed Cowpea Paste. Serve hot or cold as a snack or with any stew.

Rice

Large-scale rice cultivation in Nigeria was introduced during World War II. Different varieties suitable for most parts of Nigeria have been introduced. Essentially all rice sold in the markets for human consumption is processed white rice. Thus, most of the protein, vitamins and minerals have been removed, leaving a mainly carbohydrate product which should always be eaten with a protein-rich food. Some simple rice dishes are given here; others can be found in the Index. There are many grades of rice available in the markets. Selection should be made on the basis of quality and intended use. The polished long grain rice is best for dishes where separate grains are desirable in the cooked product. Short grain rice is often best for dishes where the rice is to be overcooked and mashed. Before buying in bulk, it is wise to try cooking a sample as badly processed rice may have an unpleasant odour and taste when cooked.

Some local rice may be infested with weevils or contain foreign materials such as sand and rice chaff. This rice will need to be cleaned carefully. It must be picked over by hand and then washed several times until the water is clean.

Simple Jollof Rice
Originally from The Gambia

Ingredients	Handy Measure	Metric
Rice	1 mgt	200 g
Stock (or 2 stock cubes in water)	2 mgt	580 ml
Onion	1 small	75 g
Fresh tomato	2 small	150 g
Fresh red pepper	2 tatasai or ata rodo	
Tomato paste	2 dsp.	18 g
Groundnut oil	3 dsp	25 ml

Clean the rice well. Grind the onion, fresh tomato and fresh pepper. Fry in oil for 5 minutes in a large cooking pot. Add the stock and tomato paste, and bring to the boil. Add the rice and turn the heat down to its lowest point. Cover tightly. When all the water has been absorbed and the grains are still separate, turn with a spoon to loosen the grains. Allow to cool partially before serving to blend the flavours. Serve with any meat, fish or chicken dish and a salad or cooked vegetable for a complete meal.

Variations Fold in $\frac{1}{2}$ mgt boiled peas or cowpeas just before serving. Add 2 mashed cloves of garlic to the fried ingredients.

Garnishing Chicken Jollof Rice

Top row (left to right): Banga soup with dry fish and snails; ripe palm fruit kernels, emilo, gbafilo, large dry cray fish, potash; land snail shells.
Bottom row (left to right): Plantain; yanghanyanghan; cooked cassava starch, green plantain pottage with goat meat.

Add ½ tsp. dried thyme, African nutmeg or curry powder with the stock. Add 2 dsp. chopped fresh spice such as tea-bush leaves or partminger.

Alternative preparation Boil 1 mgt rice with 1 mgt water until most of the water is absorbed, then add well flavoured left-over palm oil or groundnut oil stew brought to 1 mgt with water. Bring to the boil and turn down the heat. Cook covered until all the water has evaporated.

Soft Boiled Rice
Tuwo shinkafa

Ingredients	Handy Measure	Metric
Rice	3 mt	400 g
Water	7 mt	1.3 l
Salt	1 tsp	3 g

Put the rice, water and salt in a pan. Cover and cook until the rice is very soft. Mix with a wooden spoon or the back of a cooking spoon, mashing it into a firm mass. Cool partially to allow it to stiffen. It should be eaten with the fingers, accompanied by any stew, preferably one with a leafy green vegetable.

Coconut Rice

Coconut rice is prepared in many parts of the world. While some people add spices, tomato paste and other strongly flavoured ingredients, these tend to mask the coconut flavour. The colour of this coconut rice is nearly white and the coconut flavour is distinct. To give more colour and still retain the flavour, a fresh tomato and/or a fresh red pepper (seeds and membranes removed) can be sliced thinly and added with the onion.

Ingredients	Handy Measure	Metric
Rice (long grain, parboiled)	1 mgt	200 g
Coconut	1 large	1 kg
Onion	1 small	75 g
Salt	½ tsp	1.5 g
Water	2 mgt	580 ml
Tatasai, chopped finely	1 small	

Prepare coconut milk, using 2 mgt water (see Chapter 2). Bring the coconut milk to the boil and add the remaining ingredients. When the mixture is boiling, turn to the lowest heat and cover tightly. When all the water has been absorbed and the grains are still separate, turn well to loosen the grains and remove from the heat. Allow to cool partially before serving. Serve with a meat (try roasted or fried pork) or with a chicken dish and a vegetable for a very special Sunday dinner.

Variations Add 2 tsp. dry, ground crayfish, a pinch of ground cloves or 1 tsp. African black pepper.

Steamed Ground Rice I

Yoruba: *Abala*

Ingredients	Handy Measure	Metric
Rice	1 mgt	200 g
Superior palm oil	1½ dsp	15 ml
Fresh pepper	1 ata rodo	
Salt	½ tsp	1.5 g
Onion, chopped or ground	1 small	75 g
Dry crayfish, ground	½ tpt	20 g
Water	2 mgt	580 ml

Soak the rice for 30 minutes. Drain and leave to dry for 10 minutes. Beat in a mortar to a fine flour consistency and sift. You may prefer to use commercially pre-prepared rice flour, although the consistency of the final product will be different. Boil the water and add the rice flour slowly, stirring until smooth. Add the other ingredients. If necessary, add water to obtain a thick dropping consistency. Wrap in leaves and steam as for Steamed Cowpea Paste. Cool slightly before removing from leaves. Serve immediately on its own or with a meat containing stew.

Steamed Ground Rice II

Ingredients
Ground rice
Groundnut stew

Prepare ground rice or purchase commercially (see above). Mix with well-flavoured groundnut stew and water to make a thick dropping consistency. Wrap in leaves and steam as for Steamed Cowpea Paste. Serve as Steamed Ground Rice I. If meat or fish is included in the stew, cut it into small pieces.

Sweet Potato

Ipomoea batatas. Many varieties of the sweet potato are cultivated. The young leaves can be eaten and are relished by animals, but the underground tubers are the main source of food for man. The tubers may be white, red or yellow to orange. Sweet potato tubers are a valuable source of nutrients, providing in addition to carbohydrate about five per cent plant protein and substantial amounts of vitamins and minerals. Compared with the Irish potato and other West African carbohydrate sources, the sweet potato is more nourishing and it is hoped that it will become increasingly popular. As is true of most roots and tubers, many of the non-carbohydrate nutrients are more concentrated in the peel than in the pulp; cooking in the skin is therefore recommended. The skin can then be removed before serving, if desired.

To Buy Sweet potatoes do not keep well, so buy in small quantities. Check that they are firm and have no mould.

Boiled Sweet Potatoes Boil in the skin for about 25 minutes or until easily pierced with a fork. If pared before cooking, the cooking time is shortened. Season with salt and pepper before serving whole or mashed.

Baked Sweet Potatoes Wash the sweet potatoes well, then bake at 400°F, 200°C, in the oven or in charcoal or wood embers. They are done when easily pierced with a fork. If baked in coal, scrape with a knife before serving. Serve in the jacket. Excellent with pork dishes and with roast meats and fish.

Wateryam

Dioscorea alata. Wateryam is in the same family as the other yams, but is used in different ways. It is, in many parts of Nigeria, considered an inferior food to white and yellow yam. The tubers are high in water content and vary in colour from white to brown and red. Nutritionally, it has significantly more protein than other yams and more digestible carbohydrate. The peels are digestible and contain high concentrations of proteins, but are not often eaten. Wateryam is served boiled with stews. For other recipes see Index.

Fried Grated Wateryam
Yoruba: *Ojojo*

These crisp spicy balls are sold hot on the Lagos streets. They are eaten with cold eko as a light meal. They are also nice served hot as small chop, as are English potato 'chips'.

Ingredients	Handy Measure	Metric
Wateryam	2 mgt	450 g
Dry ground red pepper	1 tsp	2 g
Green onion	3 dsp	25 g
Fresh tomato, chopped	2 dsp	18 g
Salt	to taste	
Oil for frying		

Grate the wateryam finely, using the grater used for coconut. Mix in the finely chopped pepper, onion and tomato. Add salt to taste. Whip to incorporate air. Fry by dessertspoonfuls in hot oil until brown on both sides. Drain well and serve hot.
Variations Try frying in egusi seed oil. Use white onion instead of green. Use 1 chopped ata rodo instead of dry pepper. Add a little dried thyme or chopped tea-bush leaves before frying.

Wheat

Wheat is an imported grain in Nigeria. It is imported in such large quantities that several flour mills cannot keep up with the demand for the supply of flour for bread and home use. Bread is popular, particularly in urban centres, as it is purchased ready-to-eat and can be eaten with a variety of local foods to provide quick and simple meals. The vast majority of bread is white and unenriched. Until the quality of bread is improved by the addition of less processed flours of higher nutritional value, it is important for the meal-planner to see that bread meals include a protein component. Thus bread and akara or bread and tinned or dry fish would be preferable to the popular breakfast combinations of bread and dodo or bread and ogi.

If the housewife has an oven, homemade breads offer a tasty and more nutritious alternative to commercial varieties. A few suggestions for breads using flours produced from locally grown grains can be found in Chapter 10.

Another popular wheat product is Semovita (*farina*), a granular processed wheat which is used as a substitute for eba from cassava, or pounded yam. Students who travel abroad often develop recipes for eba and pounded yam with various combinations of Semovita, wheat flour, rice flour, dried potato and/or cornmeal. The nutritional value of any of these can be improved by using stocks from fish or meat as the liquid when preparing them, as is done traditionally in Lagos (see Imoyo Eba, this chapter).

Semovita Eba

Ingredients	Handy Measure	Metric
Semovita	1 mgt	150 g
Water	2½ mgt	435 ml
Salt	½ tsp	1.5 g
Vegetable oil	2 dsp	18 ml

Semovita tends to lump more easily than garri when cooking so care must be taken to mix constantly. Bring the water, salt and oil to the boil. Pour on the Semovita, stirring constantly with a wooden spoon, mashing out the lumps as they appear. The consistency should be such that it can be eaten with the fingers but not so stiff as to make it difficult to digest. The 'semo' will not thicken markedly when cooled, so that the desired consistency should be obtained before removing from the heat. If a softer product is desired, add more water; if a thicker consistency is desired, add more Semovita. To be sure the starch is cooked, continue stirring over the fire for two minutes after the last Semovita is added. Use as eba.

Yam

Dioscorea spp. The species used in Nigeria are mainly white yam (*rotundata*), yellow yam (*cayenensis*) and, to a lesser extent, trifoliate yam (*esculenta* and *dumetorium*). Yam is mainly native to Africa and is probably the oldest cultivated food here. There are innumerable varieties in Nigeria, classified locally according to shape, colour and quality of tubers. Yam is a good source of carbohydrates, and also contains some protein (4-12 per cent, depending on variety), together with some B vitamins and minerals. The varieties which are known to be good for pounding are usually higher in protein and sugar than those used for boiling. New yam which has just been harvested and old yam which has become 'soggy' are less tasty than mid-mature yam. New yam, however, has the highest quantity of protein. Other recipes using yam are available (see the Index).

To Buy It is probably wisest to ask the market woman in your locality which variety is best for your purpose. Yellow yam varieties are good for all purposes. The rusty colour that appears with peeling disappears for the most part when cooking. The best white yams for pounding may be those with long thornlike hairs, which are round and fat in shape.

Boiled Yam Yam can be washed and boiled in its skin or peeled before cooking. In either case, cut into serving-size pieces and wash. Immerse in salted water and boil covered until it can be pierced easily with a fork. Drain. Serve boiled yam with stews, fried eggs, roast meat or fish and the best grade palm oil, for any meal of the day. Unpeeled yam may be peeled before or after serving.
Variation Try boiling a mixture of green plantain, sweet potatoes, cocoyam and yam together. Each person can then select his favourite.

Pounded Yam Scrub yam, peel and cut it into chunks or slices. Place in a pot with water to cover. Cover and cook until it can be pierced easily with a fork. Pound in a mortar one piece at a time, until it forms a mass that pulls away from the sides of the mortar and is elastic to the touch. With the most powerful mixers, this can be done quite successfully, but since very little water is

used and the final product is very firm, do not try it with standard mixers. Pounding is really not as difficult as it looks, especially when small quantities are being prepared, and everyone loves pounded yam, so it is worth the effort! Pounded yam is served with soups and stews of many types at main meals.
Variation Boil some ripe plantain with the yam and pound with the yam.

Roasted Yam Wash yam well. Cut into large chunks, unpeeled. Place on glowing charcoal or on embers of firewood. When easily pierced with a fork, remove and peel. Serve with special grade palm oil, fish or meat fat, dried crayfish or simple soups and sauces. It may also be baked in the oven at 350°F, 180°C, though the pleasant smoked flavour will be lacking.

Yam Flour Wash and peel yam. Slice very thinly and leave on a piece of clean board or a stainless tray until dry (4-5 days). Grind in a flour mill. Yam flour (*elubo*) can now be purchased commercially in the market and supermarkets.

Cooked Yam Flour
Amala

Ingredients	Handy Measure	Metric
Yam flour (elubo)	1 mt	125 g
Boiling water	2 mt	580 ml

Sift the yam flour. Boil the water and set about half aside to add later. Sprinkle a little yam flour over half the water, stirring constantly with a wooden spoon to prevent lumps. Cook for 2-3 minutes, adding more hot water if necessary to get the right consistency. It should pull away from the sides of the pan but be soft in texture for eating with the fingers. Amala can be shaped on the plate with a little cold water on the hands or scooped out directly from the pot. It is often served with ewedu soup, although many other soups go well with it for a main meal. The appearance of amala puts some people off, as it is usually dark brown. The flavour, however, is not at all objectionable and some varieties of flour give a lighter product.

Yam Balls
Introduced

Ingredients	Handy Measure	Metric
Mashed cooked yam	2 mt	200 g
Eggs	1	
Groundnut oil	for deep frying	
Salt	½ tsp	1.5 g
Flour	1 tpt	45 g
Onion, chopped finely	1 small	75 g
Fresh tomato, chopped	2 dsp	15 g
Dry ground red pepper	½ tsp	1 g

Mash yam or pound in a mortar until smooth. Blend in the egg, onion, tomato, salt and pepper. Roll egg-sized balls (or smaller) in flour. Fry in deep fat until brown.

Variations Add one of the following to the yam before frying: flaked corn beef, dry thyme, fresh tea-bush leaves or partminger, some left over well-flavoured 'dry' stew or a tsp. of curry powder.

Simple Yam Pottage
Yoruba: *Ebe*

Ingredients	Handy Measure	Metric
Yam (best quality)	1 medium or six 3 cm slices, 12 cm in diameter	1 kg
Palm oil*	1 tpt or more	70 ml +
Salt	1½ tsp	4.5 g
Onion	1 medium	150 g
Fresh tomato, optional	3 medium	250 g
Fresh red pepper (ata rodo)	4 medium	12 g
Dry crayfish, ground	1 tpt	40 g

* Groundnut or other vegetable oil can be used, but if so, do not omit fresh tomato.

Peel and cut the yam into large chunks. Cover with water, adding salt and oil and bring to the boil. Grind the remaining ingredients in a mortar, blender or on a stone. Add to the yam and cook until

the yam is done. The smaller pieces may begin to break up, but the larger chunks should still be present. Stir with a wooden spoon so that more of the yam disintegrates into the soup. If a thicker pottage is preferred or the type of yam used does not thicken the liquid, some of the pieces can be 'mashed' with the back of the spoon into the sauce or puréed in a blender. Cool partially before serving to allow flavours to mix. (Serve with a leafy green stew containing meat or fish, or with roast or fried fish, snails or meat). It is also good served as a left-over the next day.
Variation   Add a handful of tea-bush leaves, a mt of prepared oil bean or 1 tsp. ground African nutmeg with the ground ingredients.

4

Meat and poultry

Meat

Nigerians eat a wider variety of meat and poultry than Europeans or Americans. In addition to the usual beef, pork, sheep and chicken, goat and undomesticated animals are popular.

Beef

Beef sold in the markets is fresh, butchered on the day of purchase. It is not cut in any particular style. 'Steak' often refers to the fillet of beef, but may refer to any large chunk of muscle. The meat has very little fat and thus tends to be tough. Since most meat is stewed, this is of little concern when cooking Nigerian foods. The supermarkets sometimes carry 'cured' beef, either imported or locally produced, which can be prepared with less cooking. Beef from the Ndama breed of cattle is more tender and finer grained than the Zebu breed, but is not often seen.

Beef which has been cut into chunks and dried (with or without heat or smoke) is popular and, when well prepared, very tasty. It is best to buy this carefully, as some dry beef may be prepared from poorly preserved meat. Before use, it should always be washed well, scrubbed with a brush and then rinsed in boiling water. Dry beef can be substituted for beef or bush-meat.

Most of the innards of beef are eaten and are often more expensive than the muscle. You must, however, get to the market early to get a good selection of tongue, liver, stomach and intestines. While local people have always appreciated the skin and cow-feet as food, the well-to-do tended to look down on them. However, in recent times they have become fashionable and they are now among the most expensive parts of the cow.

Pork

Pork is less common in the markets than beef and is more expensive. Although the large population of Muslims do not eat it, other Nigerians consider it a delicacy. The fat gives a nice flavour to plantain and yam dishes.

Sheep and Goat

Sheep and goat meat are popular and used for ceremonial occasions. To kill a sheep or goat for a religious festival or party is a mark of prestige. Cut pieces of goat are sold in the markets and are popular for special meals. When a goat or sheep is killed for an occasion in the home, all the parts are used: blood, innards, skin and flesh. Some people prefer the stronger-flavoured, old male animals, while others prefer the milder-flavoured, younger females and males.

Bush-Meat

Many types of wild animals are trapped or shot for food. They are all categorised as 'bush-meat'. Popular bush-meat includes monkey, antelope, wild pig, buffalo, grass-cutters and bats. Giant rats and dogs are also eaten as delicacies in some areas. As bush-meat is usually taken from the rural areas, where refrigeration is limited, the meat is often cooked (dried) before it is transported to local and urban markets where it fetches a high price. It is sometimes also sold along the highways.

All Meats

No matter how they are processed, all meats should be well cooked before being eaten. Husbandry methods are undeveloped for the most part and most local animals carry a variety of parasites, all of which are destroyed with prolonged cooking.

Preparation of Innards

Liver and Kidney These organs should be bought when firm, very fresh and homogenous in colour. Cut off any large blood vessels and attached membranes. Cut into chunks for boiling before adding to soups and stews. Cook thoroughly but do not overcook as the liver and kidney become hard and lose nutrients.

Intestines Wash the intestines well, inside and outside. Slit open throughout the length with a sharp knife. Remove the slimy inner coating by rubbing with fresh limes (halved) or alum (available in all markets), and wash thoroughly with cold water. Remove all the attached external membranes. The remaining intestinal wall is thin and of an uninteresting texture, so tie the intestine into knots throughout its length, until a mass of knots is produced. Cut this 'meat' into 3-5 cm chunks.

Stomach (*Rumen, reticulum, abomasum*) Wash the pieces of stomach well with cold water to remove foreign matter. Immerse in boiling water for one minute. Remove and immediately scrape the inner rough surface with the back (dull edge) of a knife, removing the dark layer. It should come off easily. Peel a thin layer of connective tissue off the outer surface. Cut the remaining 'meat' into pieces 3-4 cm.

Cowfoot, hocks The feet and hocks from cows and pigs are sold in the markets or large supermarkets, partially processed. They have been blanched and have had the hair removed. At home, they should be washed well and the larger bones which have no skin or cartilage on them discarded. The bones which have skin and cartilage should be separated into large chunks by working around them with a sharp knife. They should be just covered with salted water. Add pepper to taste. Boil for $1\frac{1}{2}$-2 hours to soften the cartilage and skin. They can then be added to any stew ten minutes before cooking time is completed. They are particularly nice with a leafy green vegetable stew. Cowfoot and hocks do not add much flavour but give an interesting texture.

Roasted Goat Meat

Large pieces of goat meat can simply be rubbed with salt and pepper and roasted over charcoal or wood fire embers. To give a special flavour, try marinading the goat meat for a few hours, preferably keeping it refrigerated. First rub the pieces of meat with limes (halved), then with a mixture of crushed garlic, dry pepper, sliced onion, salt and pepper. Roast over charcoal.

Fried Meat

Ingredients	Handy Measure	Metric
3-5 cm chunks of meat		
(beef, pork, goat, sheep)	15 pieces	450 g
Salt	1 tsp	1 g
Dry ground red pepper	1 tsp	2 g
Garlic ⎫ Optional	4 cloves	
Ginger ⎭	$\frac{1}{2}$ tsp dry	1 g
	—or fresh	

Fried meat is often prepared from meat as soon as it is brought from the market as it can then be stored for some time and used as needed for soups and stews. Fried meat is also popularly served at parties as small chop or with meatless Jollof or coconut rice. If the meat has been washed before being cut into pieces, further washing is not necessary as it would remove valuable nutrients. If, however, it was purchased in chunks, a quick rinse in cold water is advisable. Put the meat in a pot with a teaspoon of salt and add water to almost cover. Bring to the boil and then turn the heat down to its lowest point. Cover and simmer until the meat is tender and almost all the water has evaporated (40 minutes — 1 hour). A pressure cooker will cut the time in half — follow the manufacturer's instructions. Remove the meat and drain well, saving the stock for stews. Coat each piece of meat well with a mixture of salt, dry pepper, crushed garlic, and/or crushed fresh ginger to taste. Deep fry in hot fat until brown on all sides. Care should be taken here as the steam which escapes and the splattering from the water in the meat can be dangerous.

Meat Recipes

It is not possible to separate completely meat, fish, snail or even vegetable dishes, as in most dishes a combination of ingredients is used. These unusual combinations which taste right are, perhaps, among the important characteristics of Nigerian foods. Such combinations are often, nutritionally, very well balanced.

In most recipes, where a particular type of meat is specified, other types can be substituted, according to taste and availability. There are, however, certain traditional combinations and these are the ones given in the recipes.

Nigerian meals usually consist of a soup or stew and a carbohydrate. The terms soup and stew are not mutually exclusive, although stew usually refers to thicker mixtures. Pepper soups are unthickened spicy broths containing relatively large quantities of meat and/or fish to the amount of broth. Sometimes the carbohydrate is cooked in the protein dish, as in some pepper soups and in pottages, where the carbohydrate thickens the mixture.

Most meats and innards are boiled before addition to other ingredients. Except in the case of liver and kidney, a pressure cooker can be used to save time and fuel.

Simple Palm Oil or Groundnut Oil Stew with Meat

Ingredients	Handy Measure	Metric
Meat (fresh or fried)	10-15 pieces	450 g
Fresh red pepper	2 ata rodo or 2 large tatasai	
Fresh tomato	4 medium	350 g
Dry ground red pepper	1 tsp	2 g
Onion	1 large	250 g
Palm oil	½ mt	95 ml
Salt	to taste	

Cut the fresh meat into 3-5 cm chunks. Season with salt. Cover with water and boil until the meat is tender and the water has nearly evaporated. Grind the fresh pepper, tomato and onion or leave part of the onion and tomato chopped finely. Heat the oil and fry the ground ingredients for 5 minutes. Add the boiled or fried meat and dry pepper. Add salt to taste. Cook uncovered for 5 minutes stirring to prevent scorching, until nearly dry.

Today, tomato paste is often substituted for part or all of the fresh tomato, but the flavour is not as good. This is a basic stew which can be used in many ways. As there is little water, it keeps well and can be prepared in advance in large quantities for use as needed. It can be served on its own with boiled foods such as yam, cocoyam, rice or green plantain. It can also be eaten with bread or eko. It is often served with a meatless dish such as thick egusi soup, thick green stew or ewedu soup with pounded yam, eba or amala. The amount of fresh pepper, tomato and onion can be varied according to availability and taste. Groundnut or vegetable oil can be used instead of palm oil.

Beef Pepper Soup

Ingredients	Handy Measure	Metric
Beef	10-15 pieces	450 g
Dry ground red pepper	1 tsp	2 g
Onion	1 medium	150 g
Fresh tomato	2 medium	180 g
Tea-bush leaves	15-20 leaves	

Top left: Crisp fried green plantain. Centre: Suya. Top right: Boiled maize. Bottom left: Fresh coconut, boiled groundnuts in shells, roast maize. Small items (left to right): Coconut candy; chin chin; garden eggs; kulinkuli and kola nuts.

Chicken with Dodo and Salad

Ingredients	Handy Measure	Metric
African black pepper, ground	½ tsp	1 g
Dry crayfish, ground	½ tpt	10 g
Dry fish, optional	1 small	80 g
Salt	1 tsp	3 g

Cut the beef into chunks. Place in a pot and add pepper, salt and water to cover. Boil on a low heat until the meat is nearly cooked. Add extra water to cover the meat again. Add the thinly sliced or ground onion and tomato, coarsely chopped tea-bush leaves and ground dry crayfish. Add the coarsely broken dry fish if desired. Boil until the meat is cooked, at least 15 minutes. Serve hot with boiled yam or green plantain. If tea-bush leaves are not available, use any other fresh herb or dried thyme.

Banga (Palm Fruit Pulp) Soup with Beef

Ingredients	Handy Measure	Metric
Palm fruit pulp from 1 kg palm nuts (see Chapter 2)		
Beef	10-15 pieces (3 mgt)	450 g
Dry ground red pepper	1 tsp	2 g
Onion	½ small	40 g
Tomato paste	1 dsp	5 g
Fresh red pepper	4 ata rodo	
Okro	6 small	
Salt	to taste	

Make the strained palm fruit pulp up to 5 mt with water and put in a pot with the meat. Boil on a low heat until tender. Grind the onion and fresh pepper, and chop the okro finely. Add to the meat with the remaining ingredients and cook rapidly for 15 minutes, uncovered. The final cooking is best done in a local clay cooking pot as the liquid evaporates more quickly, resulting in a thicker soup without prolonged cooking. Serve with pounded yam, cooked cassava starch or tuwo.

Variation You may wish to add ½ tsp. atariko, ½ tsp. rigije, a blade of lemon grass and/or 1 dsp. beletientien to the pulp.

Simple Efo Soup with Stockfish or Meat

Ingredients	Handy Measure	Metric
Leafy greens (efo)	4 bunches	1 kg
Meat or stockfish	5-10 pieces	250 g
Fresh red pepper	12 tatasai	
Onion	1 medium	150 g
Fresh tomato	4 medium	350 g
Fermented locust bean	1 level dsp	10 g
Dry crayfish, ground	$\frac{1}{2}$ tpt	10 g
Dry red pepper	1 tsp	2 g
Palm oil or groundnut oil	for frying	
Salt	to taste	

Boil the meat, if used, in salted water until soft or, alternatively, soften the stockfish in boiling water and boil until tender. Pick the leaves over and wash thoroughly to remove grit and sand. Grind the pepper, onion, fresh pepper and tomato. Fry the cooked meat or cooked stockfish in palm oil for 2 minutes and add the ground ingredients. Chop the green leaves coarsely or finely according to taste. (The leaves should be added directly to the stew, although many housewives steep the leaves in boiling water for 3 minutes before chopping and then drain them, thus removing valuable nutrients). Add the greens to the fried stew, cover tightly and allow the steam from the wet greens to cook them. If necessary, a tpt of stock from the boiled meat or fish can be added. Cook for 5 minutes. Add the ground dry crayfish just before removing from the heat and mix well. Remove the pot from the fire and serve efo soup with eba, eko or other boiled carbohydrate.

Okro Soup with Beef and Cowpea Leaves

Ingredients	Handy Measure	Metric
Okro	12 large	250 g
Cowpea leaves	a bunch	120 g
Fresh tomato	1 large	120 g
Dry ground red pepper	1 tsp	2 g
Onion	2 medium	300 g
Salt	$1\frac{1}{2}$ tsp	4.5 g
Meat	1 mgt	230 g

Ingredients	Handy Measure	Metric
Dry fish	1 medium	280 g
Palm oil	$\frac{1}{2}$ mt	100 ml
Potash	pinch	
Ground dry crayfish, pressed	1 tpt	40 g
Ground dry ginger	$\frac{1}{2}$ tsp	1 g

Wash the meat and cut into pieces. Add onions, salt, and enough water to cover. Boil until the meat is tender and the liquid reduced by half. Add the ground tomatoes, ground crayfish, pepper, dry fish cleaned and broken into large pieces and palm oil. Cook covered for 10 minutes. Chop the okro and cowpea leaves finely and keep separate. Add cowpea leaves and okro and cook for 5-10 minutes. Serve with eba, amala, or eko.

Variation Any other leafy green vegetable can be substituted for the cowpea leaves.

Cowpea Soup with Beef and Okro
Gbegiri

Ingredients	Handy Measure	Metric
Beef (fresh or dried)	1 mt	160 g
Water	4 mt	750 ml
Cowpeas	$\frac{1}{2}$ mgt	115 g
Fresh tomato	1 medium	90 g
Fresh pepper	4 ata rodo	
Stock cube, optional	1	
Potash	pinch	
Oil (best quality palm oil)	2 tblsp	25 ml
Okro (chopped)	3 tblsp	100 g
Salt	1 tsp	3 g

Cover the meat with water in a pot and boil for 20 minutes. Meanwhile, parboil the cowpeas for 5 minutes and drain. Stir the cowpeas into the meat and continue boiling for 15 minutes. Add the ground onion, fresh pepper, tomato, potash, oil and stock cube, if used, and cook until the cowpeas are tender. Stir in the okro and cook for 3-5 minutes. Add salt to taste. Serve with tuwo or eba. If the cowpeas are hulled, the cooking time will be shortened.

Groundnut Stew

Ingredients	Handy Measure	Metric
Groundnuts	1 mt	120 g
Dry fish	1 medium	250 g
Beef	2 mgt	320 g
Fresh tomatoes	3 medium	270 g
Onion	1 medium	150 g
Garden eggs, optional	3 small	150 g
Dry ground red pepper	1 tsp	2 g
Water	2 mt	350 ml

Cut the meat into pieces and place in a pot with the chopped onion and salt. Add just enough water to cover. Add tomatoes and whole garden eggs. When the garden eggs and tomatoes are tender, remove from the soup. Grind the groundnuts (raw or roasted depending on taste) into a smooth paste. Mix with water and add to the soup. Grind the tomato and add with the dry pepper. Add dry fish and simmer until the meat is tender (about 30 minutes). Remove skin and seeds from the garden eggs and return to the soup or serve separately. Serve the soup hot with pounded or boiled yam or boiled rice.

Herbed Egusi Soup with Beef and Liver

Ingredients	Handy Measure	Metric
Beef	1 mt	160 g
Liver, kidney and/or intestines, skin, cowfoot etc.	1 mgt	230 g
Egusi seeds	1 mt	100 g
Palm oil	$\frac{1}{2}$ tpt	35 ml
Onion	1 small	75 g
Fresh pepper	2 ata rodo or 1 tatasai	
Tea-bush leaves	1 mt chopped	25 g
Salt	1 tsp	3 g
Fermented locust bean	1 dsp	10 g

Cut the beef into 3-4 cm pieces. Put in a pot with salt, intestines, skin and cowfoot etc., as used. Add water to cover the meat.

Bring to the boil and then cook over a low heat until the meat is tender and little water remains. Add water to bring the liquid up to 1 mgt. Fry the ground onion and fresh pepper in the palm oil for 5 minutes, add ground egusi seeds (roasted or unroasted according to taste) and fry for another 5 minutes, stirring well. Add the egusi mixture and the tea-bush leaves to the meat broth. Cook covered for 10 minutes. Serve with eba, fufu, pounded yam, tuwo or rice.

Liver, Yam and Ripe Plantain Pottage

Ingredients	Handy Measure	Metric
Ripe plantain, peeled	2 mgt (2 medium)	450 g
Yam	2 mgt	450 g
Fresh maize, optional	1 cob	
Liver	10-15 pieces	450 g
Groundnut oil	$\frac{1}{2}$ mt	100 ml
Fresh pepper	12 ata rodo	
Fresh tomato	3 medium	250 g
Onion	2 medium	300 g
Tomato paste	1 dsp	10 g
Partminger	1 tpt chopped	25 g
Salt	to taste	

Peel the plantain and cut into 6-8 cm pieces. Clean and peel the yam and cut into similar sized pieces. Remove kernels from maize if used. Put plantain, yam and corn into a pot and cover with water. Add salt and fresh herbs. Boil until soft. Grind onion, tomato and pepper. Fry in the oil for 10 minutes. Add liver, cut into 2-3 cm cubes. Cook for 15 minutes, adding a little water if necessary to prevent scorching. Add the liver and stew to the boiled vegetables. Mix well with a wooden spoon to blend flavours and to thicken the soup with the softened yam and plantain. Allow to cool until warm. Serve as a main meal.

Marinated Pork Cubes
Shish Kebab (introduced)

Pork cubes marinated in a lime and ginger dressing, and fried until brown and crisp or skewered and charcoal-roasted.

Ingredients	Handy Measure	Metric
Garlic	2 cloves	
Ginger, fresh	2 pieces	2.5 cm each
Onion, chopped	2 dsp	20 g
Groundnut oil	1 tpt	70 ml
Lime juice	1 tpt	70 ml
Black pepper, ground	1 tsp	2 g
Salt	1½ tsp	4.5 g
Lean pork		1 kg

Put all the ingredients except the pork in the blender or leave out the lemon juice and pound in a mortar. After pounding, add lemon juice and oil. Cut the pork into chunks, 3 cm diameter. Mix thoroughly with the marinade. Allow to marinate for 2-3 hours in the refrigerator or for 1 hour at room temperature. Heat groundnut oil (or any other vegetable oil) until it smokes and fry lightly drained pork pieces, a few at a time, until very brown and tender. Alternatively, put pork on skewers and cook over charcoal until brown and tender. Serve with Jollof rice or coconut rice and a green vegetable dish or salad.

Pork and Green Plantain Pottage

Ingredients	Handy Measure	Metric
Pork (with fat and skin)	2 mt	320 g
Green plantain	3 large	1.3 kg
African nutmeg	3 seeds	
Enge	1 pod	
Dry ground red pepper	1 tsp	2 g
Onion	1 small	75 g
Salt	to taste	

Cut the pork into large chunks 3-5 cm in diameter. Put in a pot with water to cover, adding ground African nutmeg, crushed enge, salt, pepper, thinly sliced onion and plantain, cut into thirds. Boil until the pork and green plantain are tender, turn with a wooden spoon, mashing some of the small soft pieces of plantain to thicken the broth. A few pieces of plantain can be removed with some broth, blended or pounded until smooth and returned to the pot. Season well with salt and pepper. Partially cool before

serving. Serve with starch or alone. The pottage may also be served with a green salad or lightly boiled cabbage.
Variations Substitute yam cut into large chunks or some just ripe plantain for part of the green plantain. Try substituting a tpt of chopped tea-bush leaves for the African nutmeg and enge.

Banga (Palm-fruit Pulp) Soup with Goat or Bush-meat

Prepare and serve as for Banga Soup with Dry Fish but substitute fresh goat meat, bush-meat, dry meat or a mixture of these for the dry fish. If the meat is tough, it can be parboiled in salted water before adding to the soup with the palm pulp. Three large halved or six small cooked snails and a medium sized onion, half ground and half chopped, may also be added with the pulp. A blade of lemon grass can be added with the spices.

Thin Goat Meat Pepper Soup

Ingredients	Handy Measure	Metric
Goat meat	3 mgt	480 g
Salt	1 tsp	3 g
Dry ground red pepper	1 tsp	2 g
Onion	1 small	100 g
Tea-bush leaves	1 tpt, chopped	20 g
Enge	1 pod	
Dry crayfish, ground	1 tpt	20 g
Dry fish, optional	1 small	100 g

Wash and cut the goat meat into pieces. Place in a pot and add water to cover. Add salt, pepper, thinly sliced onion and crushed enge. Boil on a low heat until the goat meat is tender. Top up water to cover and add coarsely chopped tea-bush leaves, ground dry crayfish and dry fish if used. Boil for 10 minutes. Allow to stand for 30 minutes for flavours to blend well. Reheat if necessary and serve. Serve with any boiled starchy vegetable, especially green plantain or wateryam. This is a nice supper meal, but can be eaten at any time, even for breakfast. To use as a special appetizer soup, cut the goat meat and dry fish into small bite-sized pieces of regular shape.

Thick Goat Meat Pepper Soup with Green Plantain and Yam

Ingredients	Handy Measure	Metric
Goat meat	2 mgt	480 g
Green plantain	2 medium	600 g
Yam	1 thick (3cm slice)	450 g
Salt	1½ tsp	4.5 g
Dry ground red pepper	1 tsp	3 g
Onion	1 small	75 g
Potash	pinch	
Tea-bush leaves	½ tpt pressed	12 g
Lemon grass	1 blade	
African nutmeg		2 seeds

Rinse the goat meat and cut into large chunks. Add salt, pepper and water to cover. Bring to the boil and then cook over a low heat until the meat is half cooked (about 30 minutes). Cut peeled green plantain into 3 or 4 pieces each and cut the yam into similar sized or larger pieces. Immerse in boiling water; drain. Add plantain and thinly sliced onion, chopped herbs and ground African nutmeg to the goat meat. Add enough water to cover the plantain, lifting the meat to the top to allow the plantain to sink to the bottom. Cook for another 30 minutes or until the goat meat is tender. Some of the softer plantain and yam pieces will begin to break up. These can be pressed with the back of the spoon and mixed into the broth, thickening it. If a thicker broth is desired, some pieces can be removed, mashed, pounded or blended in some of the broth and returned to the soup. Season well with salt and additional pepper to taste. Eat on its own as a complete meal or with cooked starch.

Thick Goat Meat Pottage with Green Plantain

Ingredients	Handy Measure	Metric
Goat meat	2 mgt	450 g
Green plantain	2 medium	600 g
Yam, wateryam or cocoyam	3 mgt	460 g

Ingredients	Handy Measure	Metric
Salt	1½ tsp	4.5 g
Dry red pepper, ground	1 tsp	2 g
Best grade palm oil	1 tsp	35 ml
Onion	½ tpt	1 g
Potash	pinch	
Enge, crushed	1 pod	
African nutmeg, ground	2 seeds	
Dry crayfish, ground	1 tpt pressed	40 g

Wash and cut the goat meat into large pieces. Put in a pot. Add salt, potash, enge, African nutmeg, dry pepper and just cover with water. Cover and bring to the boil, then cook over a low heat for 30 minutes. Add green plantain, cut into thirds, and yam, water-yam or cocoyam cut into similar sized chunks. Add palm oil and dry crayfish. Cook, covered, until the vegetables are soft. If some are cooked sooner than others, remove them before continuing cooking. Turn the meat and vegetables, allowing the softer ones to fragment thickening the soup, or remove a few pieces and mash or blend smoothly before returning to the pot. Season to taste with more salt and pepper. Partially cool before serving. The meat can be removed and served separately, or it can all be served in one serving dish. This pottage may be eaten with starch, alone, or with a salad or boiled cabbage for a change. This dish can also be made with pork.

Poultry

Chicken, turkey, duck and guinea fowl are available in Nigeria. Turkey and duck are not common, although some imported turkey parts are now seen in local markets. Chickens which are raised unconfined are considered to be more tasty, although they are more stringy and expensive than domesticated ones. Guinea fowl has a good flavour and is highly prized, although the meat per total weight of bird is less than in domesticated chickens. In general, the different types of poultry can be used interchangeably in the following recipes. Most chickens and guinea fowl sold in the markets are sold live. Some of the small poultry farmers now sell dressed birds, as do the supermarkets.

Fried Chicken

Fried chicken is sometimes used in soups and stews. It is commonly served at parties, often with fried beef and/or simple Jollof rice or coconut rice. If the chicken is not domesticated or you use an old layer or guinea fowl, it should be cleaned and cut into pieces and boiled before frying. Cover the chicken with water, adding salt and ground black or white pepper. Boil on a low heat for 40 minutes or until it becomes tender. Drain and then fry as for domesticated chicken. Save the broth for cooking simple Jollof rice or other soups. Domesticated local and imported chickens (fryers or broilers) do not need to be boiled before frying. Rub each piece of chicken in salt and red pepper. Place in hot fat (375°F, 190°C) and fry until brown on all sides. Drain well.

Herbed Chicken Egusi Soup

Ingredients	Handy Measure	Metric
Chicken	1 medium	1 kg
Egusi seeds (roasted or unroasted)	1 mgt	150 g
Palm oil	1 tpt	70 ml
Tea-bush leaves	2 mgt chopped	200 g
Fresh pepper	2 ata rodo or 1 tatasai	
Fresh tomato	$\frac{1}{2}$ medium	45 g
Onion	1 small	75 g
Salt	to taste	

Cut the chicken into pieces, breaking the large bones. Cover with water, add salt and boil covered on a low heat until tender and the liquid is reduced to three-quarters of its original volume. Skim off any oil on the surface and save for other uses (see Chicken Oil, Chapter 2). If unroasted egusi seeds are used, grind and fry gently in palm oil for 2 minutes; add ground tomato, onion and pepper. If roasted egusi seeds are used, add ground with all the remaining ingredients to the chicken and broth. Boil for 20 minutes, uncovered. If boiled in a clay pot, more evaporation will take place and a thicker soup will result. Serve with chicken, eba, tuwo or a boiled carbohydrate vegetable.

Nigerian Chicken Stew

Ingredients	Handy Measure	Metric
Chicken	1 medium	1 kg
Fresh tomato	4 large	450 g
Tinned tomato	½ tpt	35 g
Fresh pepper	3 ata rodo or 2 tatasai	
Onion	1 medium	150 g
Groundnut oil	½ mt	100 ml
Salt	to taste	
Dry ground red pepper	to taste	

Boil the chicken almost covered in salted water. If using a broiling chicken, cook for 10 minutes. If using an old layer or undomesticated chicken, cook for 30 minutes. Meanwhile, grind the tomato, fresh pepper and onion and fry in groundnut or other vegetable oil until almost dry. Add to the boiled chicken. Cook uncovered for 15 minutes or until the chicken is tender. Serve for a special meal with boiled white rice and dodo.
Variations Add 1 dsp. curry powder with the ground tomato. Add 1 tsp. dried thyme or a handful of chopped fresh herbs.

Chicken Pepper Soup

A speciality of Miriam's mother-in-law who mixes undomesticated with domesticated chickens for flavour and economy.

Ingredients	Handy Measure	Metric
Chicken	1 medium	1 kg
Fresh tomato	2 medium	180 g
Onion	1 small	75 g
Dry pepper	1½ tsp	3 g
Enge	1 pod	
Salt	to taste	

Clean and cut the chicken; break the large bones and include all the edible innards. Grind the tomato and onion, crush the enge and add with the dry pepper to the chicken. Add enough water to cover and bring to the boil. Lower the heat and simmer, covered, until the chicken is tender. Serve plantain and chicken pepper soup separately for any meal, including breakfast. This soup tastes better if prepared a few hours in advance and is then reheated just before use.

Banga (Palm Fruit Pulp) Soup with Chicken

Prepare and serve as Banga (Palm Fruit Pulp) Soup with Dry Fish but substitute a partially cooked (in salted water to cover) cut up chicken for the dry fish and dry crawfish. Omit the okro, but add one medium onion (half ground, half chopped), a blade of lemon grass and the chicken broth with the palm pulp. Three large or six small snails can also be added.

Imoyo Chicken
Chicken in Marinade

Ingredients	Handy Measure	Metric
Chicken	1 medium	1 kg
Okro	5 medium	75 g
Onion	1 medium	150 g
Garlic	2 cloves	
Fresh tomato	5 small	250 g
Tomato paste	1 dsp	10 g
Fresh pepper	5 ata rodo or 3 tatasai	
Vinegar	$1\frac{1}{2}$ dsp	12 ml
Olive oil	3 dsp	18 ml
Salt	to taste	

Clean and cut up the chicken into serving-size pieces. Cover with water in a pot and bring slowly to the boil. Boil on a low heat until tender. Remove 1 mt of broth and cook the halved fresh tomato, quartered onion, whole okro, fresh pepper (with seeds and membranes removed) and crushed garlic in it for 5 minutes, uncovered. Drain the chicken, reserving the stock for Imoyo Eba. Add tomato purée, vinegar and olive oil to the boiled vegetables, mixing gently with a spoon. Pour over the chicken and allow to marinate for an hour or more. Serve warm with Imoyo eba. Vegetable oil can be used instead of olive oil.

Chicken and Okro Soup

Ingredients	Handy Measure	Metric
Chicken	1 medium	1 kg
Onion, chopped	1 small	75 g
Okro	18 large	300 g
Dry ground red pepper	1 tsp	2 g
Dry crayfish, ground	1 tpt	40 g
Fresh tomato	2 medium	180 g
Tomato paste	2 dsp	18 g
Salt	to taste	1.5 g
Potash, ground	$\frac{1}{2}$ tsp	

Clean and cut the chicken into pieces, breaking the bones. Place in a pot with salt and pepper, cover with water and boil until tender. Drain, reserving the broth. Grate the okro coarsely and add it with the remaining ingredients. Boil for 5 minutes. Return the chicken to the pot and continue to cook for 5 minutes more. Serve with eko, eba or tuwo.

Variation Add some cooked ewedu or washed bitter leaf with the okro. If the chicken is lean, 3 dsp. oil may be added.

Nigerian Curried Chicken

Ingredients	Handy Measure	Metric
Chicken, cut up	1 medium	1 kg
Vegetable oil	$\frac{1}{2}$ mt	90 ml
Onion	2 medium	300 g
Fresh pepper	3 ata rodo or 1 tatasai	
Fresh tomato	3 large	360 g
Curry powder	3 dsp	25 g
Flour	1 tpt	40 g
Salt	to taste	
Stock cubes, optional	2	

Cover the chicken in salted water and boil until half cooked (15 minutes for a broiler and 30 minutes for an undomesticated chicken). Fry the finely chopped onion until soft; add curry powder and fry for 1 minute. Add ground tomato, pepper and stock cubes, if used, to the boiling chicken. Boil uncovered until the chicken is tender. Salt to taste. Blend the flour with a few large kitchen spoons of broth, blending until smooth, then add to the chicken. Boil for 10 minutes. Serve with rice.

Curry accompaniments Diced pawpaw, diced pineapple, ground dry crayfish, ground ginger, grated fresh or roasted coconut, fried ripe plantain in small cubes, sliced guava, finely chopped raw onion, fried onions, chopped tomato, chopped fresh pepper (with seeds and membranes removed), sliced bananas, whole dry crayfish (with heads and tails removed).

Chicken Jollof Rice

Ingredients	Handy Measure	Metric
Rice	2 mgt	400 g
Chicken	1 medium	1 kg
Fresh tomato	4 large	450 g
Tinned tomato, optional	½ tpt	35 g
Onion	1 medium	150 g
Fresh red pepper	1 ata rodo	
African black pepper, ground, optional	1 tsp	2 g
Salt	1½ tsp	4.5 g
Vegetable oil	½ tpt	35 ml

If an undomesticated chicken, old layer or guinea fowl is used, the chicken should be covered with salted water and boiled until half cooked before adding to the rice. Vegetable oil should be used.

If the chicken is of a tender broiling or frying type, it can be cooked directly with the rice and no vegetable oil will be needed. Grind the onion, tomato and fresh pepper. Make up to 4 mgt by adding chicken broth or water. Bring all the ingredients except the rice to the boil. Add the rice and chicken and return to the boil. Turn the heat to its lowest point and cover tightly. Cook until all the liquid is absorbed and the chicken is tender. Turn the Jollof rice gently to loosen the rice grains and then cover it again and allow to rest for an hour to blend the flavours well. Serve with dodo as a special occasion meal. Try adding a vegetable salad to this combination.

5

Fish and shellfish

The most important source of animal protein in the majority of Nigerian homes is fish and shellfish. Even meals which are considered by the cook to have no meat or fish will often be 'spiced' with ground dry crayfish or ground fish.

Fish protein has a high nutritional value and is, therefore, an important part of a good balanced diet. In addition to being a valuable source of protein, essential vitamins and minerals are also present. Fish protein, well prepared, is relatively easy to digest, making it invaluable for children and invalids. It is also low in calories and, therefore, ideal in weight reducing diets.

Nigeria has a wide variety of fish from both fresh water and the ocean. Fresh fish and shellfish are available at the coasts and lakesides and some varieties, which can survive for long periods out of water, are even available from inland markets. Frozen fish, packed at sea or from the big lakes and rivers, are distributed through cold stores. However, the most readily available fish are those which have been preserved by heating and smoking: the so-called 'dry-fish'.

Fresh fish

More than 200 species of fish are caught in the various aquatic habitats of Nigeria. In local markets near their source, live, fresh fish are available daily. However, being highly perishable and caught under difficult conditions, often with ingenious technology, by a decreasing population of individual private fishermen, they are expensive. Indeed, one is likely to pay more for a fresh fish than a processed 'dry-fish' of equal size. Varieties available

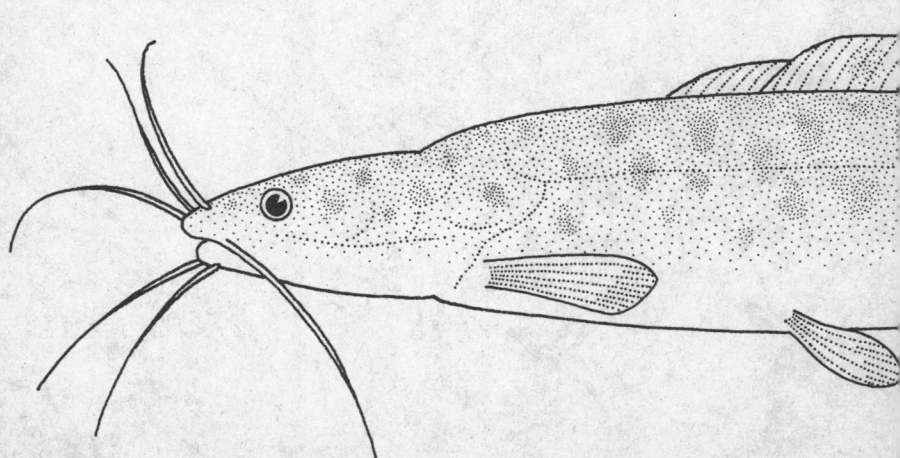

depend on the location and season, but a few are widespread and available all the year round. Except for the *Claridae*, all fresh fish should be bought and cleaned as soon as possible after they are caught and either cooked quickly or frozen until needed. Clarias, however, is a kind of mudfish, related to the catfish, which survives for long periods away from water and can be carried home live and kept for some days in a bucket of water. It is, however, a very strong and active fish and may find its way out of the most cleverly devised container! The head is a large proportion of the fish, so the larger sized types are perhaps the most economical unless, of course, you relish the head, as many people do. While this fish can be cooked and eaten directly (it has few bones and a very 'meaty' dense flesh), it is more commonly smoked or roasted before cooking.

Fresh fish should be purchased with care. The eyes should be clear and bulging, the gills bright pink-red and the flesh firm; there should be no 'fishy' smell. While there has been some fear about localised use of pesticides for killing fish, this method is confined to small bodies of water. Most fish killed in this way are used locally and do not reach the urban markets.

Medium and large size fish are cleaned by removing the innards (the roe is retained for eating, as well as the intestines of certain types in some areas) and scaling and trimming the fins and tail if desired. The head may be cut off when cleaning, but it is usually retained for the stew or soup as it imparts extra flavour. Small fish can be simply gutted before eating; sprats and other tiny fish are often eaten whole.

If fresh fish are not to be eaten immediately, it is best to freeze, fry or boil them and refrigerate, or alternatively, smoke and roast them.

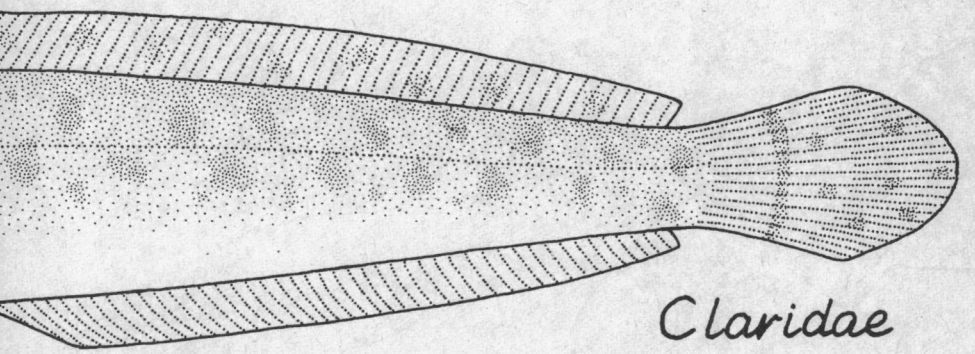

Claridae

Frozen fish

There was a time when people to whom fresh fish had always been available would not eat frozen 'ice-fish' as it is called in Nigeria. If you asked a waterside dweller how times were treating him and all was not well, he would tell you: 'we now eat ice-fish in our house!' No one who has eaten fish cooked fresh from the water will pretend that it can be replaced by a defrosted frozen one! However, the modern methods of fresh-freezing and storing provide a high quality product at a reasonable price which is readily and regularly available in most local markets.

The most common types of frozen fish available all the year round are varieties of mackerel and horse mackerel. These are related to the tuna fish, which is also occasionally seen for sale in the markets in slices. Seasonally, bream, ladyfish, croaker, barracuda, eel and sprats are available from the sea. Niger perch is sometimes available from coldstores, brought from Lake Chad and the River Niger. More varieties are available in the supermarkets than in the local open markets, but at substantially greater cost. Mackerel and related varieties are oily and many Nigerians prefer to smoke or roast them to drain off the oil, before storing them for use.

Smoked roast fish (Dry fish)

Fish which has been preserved by heat is generally referred to as 'dry fish'. This term, however, is misleading as 'dry fish' includes fish which:

a) has been lightly smoked to give flavour only but is essentially 'raw';
b) has been smoked and roasted or heated thoroughly, so that it is, in fact, cooked and can be eaten directly;
c) has been dried completely over charcoal or woodfire until it is crisp and can be kept safely for weeks.

Most 'dry fish' is of type (b): that is, while it has been heated enough to cook it, it is still moist and, therefore, highly perishable. Dry fish is readily susceptible to infection by flies. The flies lay their eggs on the fish, and these hatch into larvae, which decompose the fish flesh giving it a characteristic odour. Such fish is still sold, often after the market woman has re-heated it to dry it further and thus masked its smell and, indeed, it is commonly eaten. This is tolerable as the fish is first cleaned well and over-cooked in most dishes. Fish salvaged in this way is not, however, the special treat that a well-smoked fish is. In order to buy good uninfected smoked fish, each piece must be observed carefully for any sign of deterioration (check especially around large bones) dampness, maggots and smell. A good smoked fish will have a pleasant 'sweet' smoked scent.

If one is unfortunate enough to bring home what turns out to be an infected fish or piece of fish, and this happens to the most experienced cook occasionally, try breaking the fish into large chunks, washing well (removing maggots if present) and drying in the oven (at 225°F, 110°C) or over a charcoal or wood fire. This may take a few hours and will reduce the smoked fish flavour, but will eliminate the 'spoiled' odour and taste.

'Dry fish' is prepared over charcoal or firewood; the fire may provide heat, or heat and smoke, imparting a scent characteristic of the type of wood used. Thus, 'roasted' fish is probably the most correct term, though to some this may imply over-baking. We

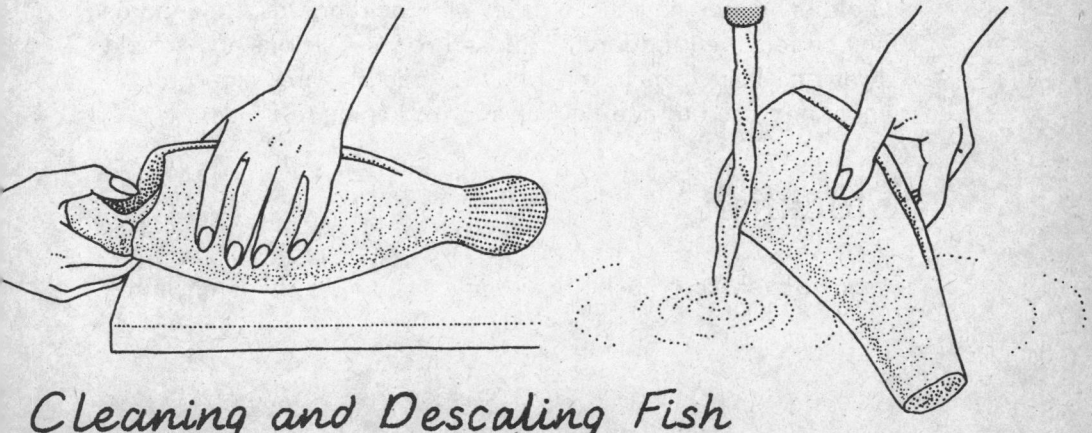

Cleaning and Descaling Fish

will, therefore, use the common term 'dry fish' for all heat-processed fish. In most recipes, fish of various degrees of processing can be used interchangeably; when one type is preferred, it will be noted.

A poor substitute for charcoal or wood fire processing can be achieved by oven-roasting fish or pieces of fish on a rack over a drip pan in a very low oven, (225-250°F, 110°C), until most of the juices or oils have evaporated or drained from the fish. Before roasting, rub the fish lightly with oil (palm oil or groundnut oil), salt, and dry pepper. Use this dry roasted fish where dry fish is called for in cooking.

All varieties of fish are dried. The most common types seen in the markets are clarias (of various sizes), Niger perch (in large chunks), tilapia, herring and mackerel, and various tiny fish, including sprats (see the table below).

Dry fish can be kept in hanging baskets devised for keeping foods well ventilated, but away from pests. Such baskets are adequate for dry season storage, but during the wet season they should be hung over the hearth or the fish removed and re-heated periodically to prevent spoilage. If dry fish is kept in the refrigerator, it tends to take up moisture and spoilage occurs, although more slowly than at room temperature. It is probably best, particularly if buying large quantities of dry fish, to re-heat it in the oven or over an open fire to sterilise it. Then it should be stored in airtight containers or plastic bags in the refrigerator or, better still, in the freezing compartment.

When cleaning dry fish, they should be scrubbed well to remove sand and ash. Then they are broken into large pieces, immersed in boiling water and again washed. Some debris settles; other debris floats; both are discarded. The chunks of fish flesh, skin, large bones and head are retained for cooking and are referred to as 'dressed dry fish'. Smaller dry fish may be eaten whole or, if they have been dried with their innards, the innards may be removed if desired. Smoked roe is delicious and should always be kept. Small dry fish, like crayfish, are often ground whole and used to add flavour and thickening to foods.

Stockfish

Panla; okporoko; Stockfish, completely dried fish, is an intro-

Varieties of dry fish

Name or type	Weight as usually purchased	Weight when dressed	How to clean	Comments
Clarias (mudfish)	Wide variation in size: e.g. medium one: 200 g	185 g 150 g excl. head	Wash, scrub well. Break open and remove any innards, soft matter in head, and bones, if desired.	Sold part to very dry
Niger perch and other large fresh water fish	Sold in chunks of flesh; little bone.	125 g or more	Wash well; break open around bones. Wash large pieces	Usually light to medium dry
Herring, 'Sardine', Bonga fish, Sawa (smaller), Agobodo (bigger)	1 medium: 25 g	12 g	Remove head, fins, tail innards and skin and use only the inner flesh. Or, eat whole, particularly the smaller ones	Sold very dry
White bait (sprats), yoyo etc.			Eat whole	Sold very dry. Eat whole or ground
Tilapia and other medium scaled fish	1 medium: 35 g	20 g	Remove head and any innards left. Wash and cook head and body	Very dry. Market women who sell fresh fish often dry it when it appears to be 'going off'; select carefully
Mackerel, horse fish etc.	Wide range of size, up to 1500 g		Remove innards if necessary; wash. Bones easily removed after cooking	Little waste. Usually part dried from ice fish by the fish sellers themselves

duced, imported food, which is extremely popular throughout Nigeria. It is important because of its excellent keeping qualities. It is imported in vast quantities and in years past was economical, though at present it is rather expensive, probably due to some restriction on import quantities. While stockfish does not add a lot of flavour to a dish, it does provide protein and gives 'something to chew on'. It is usually best to have the stockfish cut into pieces with an electric saw in the market for a few kobos, as it is difficult to cut with a knife when dry. Before use, it can be soaked in hot water for thirty minutes or more or boiled until softened to taste. Then it is added to the food being prepared.

Shellfish

Fresh shellfish are available only near their habitats as they are extremely perishable. Care must be taken when buying them to ensure that they are alive. Clams, oysters, periwinkles, shrimps and prawns are usually available and are sold, shelled, by the cup. Crabs and lobsters should be alive and active. Periwinkles stay alive for long periods out of water as they form a membrane over the opening into the shell, which prevents dehydration.

Frozen and chilled shellfish are not widely available. However, frozen shrimps and prawns are becoming more common and, occasionally, frozen crabs are seen.

Dried shellfish (smoked and roasted) are more widely available. Smoked clams, oysters and periwinkles are tasty and add interest to many fresh or dry fish dishes. Dry crayfish (actually dried or roasted and smoked shrimps and prawns) are almost universally used in Nigerian cookery. Shrimp is available in a lighter form (sun-dried) and a reddish-brown form (smoked and roasted). Both are added to stews ground or whole after heads, tails and legs (which can all be ground and added to the food as well) have been removed. The large-sized dry crayfish are added to foods after the head, tail and legs are removed; the shell is edible. When washed and re-dried, all dry shellfish are tasty as finger food.

Land crabs and fresh water crayfish are available in some localities. Fresh water crayfish are sometimes available alive, but are more often sold boiled or dried. They have less flavour than salt water crayfish but have an interesting texture.

Sprats in Groundnut Oil Stew
Yoruba: *Yoyo stew*

Whole crisp quick-fried sprats tossed in a rich pepper, tomato and oil stew.

Ingredients	Handy Measure	Metric
Sprats	2 mgt	450 g
Onion	1 small	75 g
Fresh tomato	4 medium	360 g
Fresh red pepper, ground	1 ata rodo or 1 tatasai	
Groundnut oil	2 mgt	580 ml
Salt	1 dsp	9 g
African black pepper, ground	1 tsp	2 g
Tomato paste	½ tpt (small tin)	35 g

Clean the sprats with water, removing innards only if desired. Season with salt and black pepper. Grind tomatoes, onion and peppers. Heat the groundnut oil until it smokes and fry sprats in small amounts for 1-2 minutes or until brown. Set sprats aside. Strain half of the oil into another pot. Add the ground peppers, onions, tomatoes and tomato paste. Fry thoroughly until almost dry (15 minutes or longer). Toss sprats in the stew and serve.
Comments This dish travels well. It can be served with boiled foods or leafy green stews and a thickened carbohydrate food such as eba or pounded yam.

Fried Whitebait or Sprats
Yoruba: *Yoyo Salapore*

Tiny crisp-fried fish, eaten whole as a snack or as part of a meal.

Ingredients	Handy Measure	Metric
Whitebait or sprats	4 mgt	900 g
Groundnut oil or palm oil for frying		
Wheat flour (white)	1 mt	125 g
Dry ground red pepper	1 tsp	2 g
Salt	1½ tsp	4.5 g

Wash the fish carefully; drain and dry with a clean cloth. Toss the well-drained fish in a mixture of flour, pepper and salt. Shake off the excess flour. Heat the oil until it smokes; add the fish, a handful at a time, and cook quickly until crisp and brown. This takes only a few minutes. Do not put too many fish in the pot at one time or the oil will cool and the fish become soggy and oil-soaked.

Fresh Fish Palm Oil or Groundnut Oil Stew

Whole slices of fresh fish in a simple red stew, flavoured with fresh red pepper.

Ingredients	Handy Measure	Metric
Fresh fish (any type)	2 medium	500 g
Large red fresh pepper	4-6 tatasai	
Tomato paste	1 dsp	10 g
Onion	1 small	75 g
Fresh tomato	1 small	60 g
Palm oil or groundnut oil	$\frac{1}{2}$ tpt	35 ml
Salt	to taste	
African black pepper, optional	to taste	

Clean the fish and cut into serving-size pieces. Season with salt and pepper. Grind peppers, $\frac{1}{2}$ onion and tomato paste together. Slice remaining $\frac{1}{2}$ onion and tomato very thinly. Heat the oil until it smokes. Fry the ground peppers, $\frac{1}{2}$ onion and tomato with tomato paste until they are cooked but not browned, stirring constantly near the end when all the water will have boiled off. Add 1 mgt (270 ml) of water and bring to the boil. Add the fish, sliced $\frac{1}{2}$ onion and thinly sliced tomato. Simmer until the fish is cooked (about 10 minutes). Add salt to taste. Use a spoon or shake the saucepan to prevent breaking up the fish. Serve with boiled rice, boiled yam, boiled plantain and/or beans.

Variations Instead of using fresh fish alone, a combination of fresh fish, crabs and fresh shrimps may be used.

Imoyo Eleja
Fresh Fish in Marinade

This is a recipe of Brazilian origin, popular among Lagos indi-

FISH AND SHELLFISH

genes. It has chunks of boned fish in a chopped tomato, onion and fresh pepper marinade spiced with garlic and African black pepper, tossed in a light oil, vinegar and stock dressing.

Ingredients	Handy Measure	Metric
Fresh or frozen fish (croaker, ladyfish, mackerel, etc.)		500 g
Fresh prawns, if desired	10	
Vinegar or lime juice	2 dsp	18 ml
Fresh red pepper	1-2 ata rodo	
Ground dry pepper, optional	1 tsp	
Fresh tomato	1 medium	90 g
Onion	1 medium	150 g
Olive oil or cooked groundnut oil	1 tpt	70 ml
Garlic	3 cloves	
Tomato paste	$\frac{1}{2}$ tpt	35 g
African black pepper corns	1 tsp	2 g
Salt	to taste	

Disinfect the tomatoes and fresh pepper, as they are to be eaten raw (see salads, Chapter 7). Clean and scale fish, trimming fins and tail, then cut into slices 5 cm thick, saving the head. Finely chop the onion, red fresh pepper (removing membranes and seeds), garlic and tomatoes. Mix together except for the garlic. If groundnut oil is used, heat it until it smokes and then cool. Grind the African black pepper using a mortar or stone. Season the fish slices, including the head, with salt, pepper, chopped garlic and black pepper. Just cover the fish with water adding shelled prawns, if used. Cook until done (7-10 minutes). Remove fish and prawns carefully and allow to cool on a plate, saving the stock. While the fish is cooking, soak the onions, fresh pepper and tomatoes in the oil and vinegar. Remove the bones from the fish and break up the flesh into bite-sized chunks. Mix the marinated tomatoes, onions and peppers with the tomato paste and $\frac{1}{2}$ mgt (135 ml) sieved stock. Add the dry pepper, if used. Then mix in the fish pieces and prawns, taking care not to break up the fish further. Season with salt.

This dish can be eaten immediately or refrigerated for a few hours to bring out the flavour. Traditionally it is served with Imoyo Eba, prepared with the remaining fish stock. It may also be served with rice, coconut rice or as an appetizer with rolls or toast. It is nice served on lettuce leaves or with grated cabbage.

Banga (Palm Fruit Pulp) Soup with Fresh Sea Foods

Prepare and serve as Banga Soup with Dry Fish but substitute fresh fish (2 medium, 500 g), periwinkles (1 mt, dressed, removing the hard 'eye' and soft intestine if desired), and fresh shrimps, shelled or unshelled with heads removed (1 mgt), for the dry fish and dry crayfish. Add the fresh fish towards the end of the cooking so that it does not break up. Fresh clean crabs can also be added if available.

Dry Fish, Fresh Fish and Dry Okro Soup
Northern Nigeria: *Kuka soup*

A light fish soup with little oil thickened slightly with dry ground okro.

Ingredients	Handy Measure	Metric
Dry ground okro (nuru)	1 dsp	10 g
Fresh red pepper	1 medium ata rodo	
Fresh tomato	1 medium	90 g
Onion	½ medium	75 g
Palm oil	½ tpt	35 ml
Dry fish or fresh (or both)	one small dry fish or one small fresh fish	300 g
Salt	to taste	

Grind the pepper, tomato and onion. Clean the fish and cut into large pieces. If using fresh fish, rub with salt and dry red pepper. Mix the ground tomato, onion and peppers with 2 mgt water. Add the palm oil and boil for 15 minutes, uncovered. Add the dry fish and/or fresh fish and boil, covered, for 10 minutes or longer on a low heat. Sieve the okro and add to the soup. Boil for 10 minutes on a low heat, stirring gently to prevent scorching. This soup is traditionally served with tuwo, fufu or other thickened carbohydrate food. It can be eaten at breakfast, lunch or dinner. You can buy the prepared dried okro in the market.

Fresh Fish and Prawn Pepper Soup
Itsekiri: *Gbagba;* Ijaw: *Igina Fulou*

Fresh fish and prawns in a highly seasoned thin soup. There is no oil in this tasty aromatic dish.

Ingredients	Handy Measure	Metric
*Spices		
African nutmeg	4 seeds, roasted	
Emilo	$\frac{1}{2}$ seed	
Gbafilo	$\frac{1}{4}$ seed	
Enge	1 pod	
Yanghanyanghan (pulp only)		2 cm piece
*Herbs		
Lemon grass and/or	1 blade	
Tea-bush leaves	4-5 leaves	
Other ingredients		
Dry ground red pepper	1 tsp	3 g +
Salt	1 dsp	
Fresh fish	1 medium	500 g
Fresh shrimps or prawns	1 mt	150 g

The following ingredients were not traditionally included, but are often included when available today:

Fresh tomato	1 medium	90 g
Onion	$\frac{1}{4}$ medium	40 g
Fresh red pepper	1 ata rodo	1
	$\frac{1}{2}$ tatasai	$\frac{1}{2}$

*The dry spices and herbs can be used in various combinations; if any one is not available, prepare the soup without it.

Clean and wash the fish, cut into 3-4 cm slices and rub with salt. Remove seeds from the enge and add the pod to the other spices. Grind the spices in a mortar or with a stone. Grind onion, tomato and fresh pepper. Boil all the ingredients except the fish and shrimps in 2 mgt (540 ml) water for 10 minutes. Add the fish and shrimps. Cook on a medium heat with the cover off until the quantity is reduced by half.

Comments Pepper soups are generally cooked down to concentrate the flavour; the fish will then make up more than half the volume. A small amount of this flavourful soup is served per person, but because it is concentrated it can be used with a full serving of carbohydrate. Pepper soup can be served with boiled yam or boiled unripe plantain. It is also nice with rice, or as an appetizer in a formal meal.

Grated Cocoyam in Leaves with Dry Fish and Meat
Efik: *Ekpan Nkukwo*

This is a *very* rich dish, but tasty and interesting in appearance and texture. Definitely not for weight-watchers.

Ingredients	Handy Measure	Metric
Young tender leaves of large size (cocoyam, red stemmed variety, ugwu, tete, etc.)	1 large 'bunch'	300 g
Dry fish, cleaned	1 medium	250 g
Dry crayfish, small size	2 mt	75 g
Onion	1 medium	150 g
Fresh tomato	2 medium	180 g
Dry ground red pepper	2 tsp	4 g
Beef or goat meat	1 mgt	225 g
Cocoyam or wateryam, grated	3 mgt	600 g
Salt	1½ tsp	4.5 g
Palm oil, best quality	½ mt	100 ml

Boil the meat in chunks in water to cover. Season with salt and pepper. Remove the heads and tails from the dry crayfish and grind. Grind the onion and tomato. Wash the leaves well and use whole or tear the larger ones into hand-sized pieces. Mix the grated cocoyam with ½ tsp. salt (1.5 g). Hold a leaf in one hand, place a heaped dsp. of grated cocoyam in the lower third and wrap the leaf around it in a tube. Lay the wrapped cocoyam parcel in the bottom of a large oiled cooking pot. Continue until all the cocoyam is wrapped. Lay the chunks of dry fish and cooked meat on top. Mix the broth from boiling the meat, the whole and ground dry crayfish, the ground tomato and onion, and pour over the top. Then pour the oil over. Bring to a boil, cover tightly and turn down the heat. After 10 minutes check to see that the stew is not scorching. If it appears to be getting dry, a tpt of water should be added. Continue to cook for 20 minutes more. Turn the contents gently with a large spoon. Some of the cocoyam parcels will have broken up, the contents thickening the stew; others will remain formed. Re-cover, lower the heat and cook carefully for 15 minutes to blend the flavours well. Partially cool and serve. This is a one course meal.

Agbono with Fresh Fish and Locust Bean Stew

Afemai method

Ingredients	Handy Measure	Metric
Fresh fish	1 medium	450 g
Agbono	15 pieces	12 g
Dry ground red pepper	1 tsp	2 g
Onion	1 small	75 g
Fresh tomato	2 medium	180 g
Palm oil	$\frac{1}{2}$ tpt	35 ml
Fermented locust beans	1 dsp	10 g
Dry crayfish, small size	1 mt	40 g
Salt	to taste	
Potash, optional	pinch	

Grind the agbono with a little palm oil in a mortar or without oil in an electric grinder. Clean the fish and cut it into large serving size pieces. Grind the pepper, onion, tomato and crayfish. Put the palm oil, potash and 2 mgt water in a pot. Bring to the boil. Add all the other ingredients except the fish and boil for 20 minutes on a low heat. Add the fish and cook until tender, stirring gently to prevent breaking it. Serve with pounded yam, eba or amala.

Stewed Greens with Dry Fish

Efik: *Edikan Ikon*; Yoruba: *Efo riro*

Greens in a well-flavoured dry palm oil stew with a variety of seafood for texture and flavour.

Ingredients	Handy Measure	Metric
Firm leaves (try ugu, soko etc.)	6 mgt (3 'bunches')	600 g
Onion	1 large	250 g
Fresh tomato	2 large	240 g
Fresh pepper	4 ata rodo	
Dry fish	1 medium	250 g
Stockfish	4 pieces	150 g
Dry crayfish, small size	2 mgt	100 g
Dry crayfish, large size	1 mgt	50 g
Salt	to taste	
Palm oil (best quality)	½ mt	100 ml
Water leaf	2 mgt	200 g
Boiled meat	5-10 pieces	250 g
Periwinkles in shell } optional	2-3 dozen	
Snails, dressed	3-4 large	900 g

Pick over leaves and wash well. Chop or slice finely. Boil pieces of stockfish until tender. Grind small dry crayfish and remove heads, tails and legs of large dry crayfish (these may be ground with the crayfish if desired). Grind tomato, onion and fresh pepper. Clean and boil snails if used (see Chapter 6) and boil meat in large chunks until tender. Fry the palm oil until hot but not smoking; add ground tomato, onion, pepper and stockfish (together with snails and meat, if used). Simmer for 20 minutes. Sprinkle on dry ground crayfish and put the dry fish, large dry crayfish and periwinkles, if used, on top. Cover and cook for 15 minutes adding only enough water to prevent scorching. Put the greens on top and cover the pot. Allow to 'wilt', then remove cover and begin to turn the stew gently. Avoid breaking up the dry fish. It can be removed before adding the greens and served on top of the stew in the serving dish. Add a few drops of water, if necessary, to prevent scorching the greens. Some water will come out of the greens as they cook and this, together with the oil coating the pan, will help to prevent burning. The stew will be very thick, with very little water, the greens being held together by the oil.

Serve with well-prepared fufu, pounded yam or even boiled rice. This dish is also tasty served with fried dodo for supper or with boiled yam.

Dry Okro and Groundnut Fish Soup

Ingredients	Handy Measure	Metric
Dried okro	1 tpt	20 g
Fresh or dry fish	1 medium	250 g
Groundnut oil	1 tpt	70 ml
Groundnuts	1 tpt	50 g
Greens (try soko, ugu, etc.)	1 mt	150 g
Onion	1 medium	200 g
Fresh tomato	2 medium	180 g
Dry, ground red pepper	1 tsp	2 g
Salt	to taste	

Pound dried okro in a mortar or buy already ground (use 3 dsp). Wash and cut the greens finely. Clean the fish. Boil 2 mt water, groundnut oil and ground groundnuts for 5 minutes. Parboil (steam) greens in another pot with a minimum of water for 5 minutes. Add the onion, tomato and pepper to the groundnuts, oil and water. Boil for 15 minutes. Add the dried okro, greens and fish. Cook gently so as not to break up the fish until the fish is done (about 15 minutes). Mix gently. Served with eko or any thickened carbohydrate food.

Banga (Palm-fruit Pulp) Soup with Dry Fish
Itsikiri: *Obe Eyen*

Ingredients	Handy Measure	Metric
Palm fruits	2 congos	1.5 kg
Atariko, ground	1 tsp	2 g
Rigije, ground	$\frac{1}{2}$ tsp	1 g
Dry ground red pepper	1-2 tsp	2-4 g
Salt	$1\frac{1}{2}$ tsp	4.5 g
Dry whole crayfish, small size	2 mt	35 g
Dry ground crayfish	1 tpt	40 g
Okro, ground or chopped	1 tpt	35 g
Potash, optional	$\frac{1}{2}$ tsp	1.5 g
Ground beletientien	2 dsp	5 g

Prepare palm fruit as directed in Chapter 2, producing about 2 litres of pulp. Add atariko, rigije, dry pepper and salt. Sprinkle beletientien over the soup and bring to the boil. Add ground and whole dry crayfish with heads and tails removed, okro and potash, if used. Boil uncovered, preferably in a locally made clay pot which facilitates evaporation, until the volume is reduced by almost half. Add the dry fish and cook for another 20 minutes. Banga soups are preferred by some rather watery, and by others very thick. Serve with boiled foods or thickened carbohydrate foods, particularly cassava starch.

Imitation Banga Soup with Dry Fish

Ingredients	Handy Measure	Metric
Rigije, ground	1 tsp	2 g
Atariko	½ tsp	1 g
Beletientien	1 dsp	3 g
Snails	6 large or 12 small	
Periwinkles, shelled	1 mgt	250 g
Dry fish, dressed	1 medium	150 g
Dry crayfish, large, whole	1 mt	50
Dry crayfish, small, ground	1 tpt	40
Crayfish eggs, optional	1 dsp	2 g
Water	3 mgt	870 ml
Onion	1 small	100 g
Okro, grated	3 medium	100 g
Salt	1½ tsp	4.5 g
Potash, ground	¼ tsp	1 g
Dry, ground red pepper	1-2 tsp	2-4 g
Flour (white, wheat)	½ tpt	40 g

Grind rigije and atariko. Clean and dress the snails and cook snails covered with salted water until tender. Remove 'eye' and intestine from periwinkles if desired. Clean dry fish. Grind heads and tails from large crayfish with the small ones. Bring oil, water, rigije, atariko, dry crayfish (whole and ground), crayfish eggs, if used, potash, salt and dry pepper to the boil. Add periwinkles, snails and dry fish. Sprinkle the belentientien over the boiling soup and simmer uncovered for 30 minutes. Add the okro and boil for 10 minutes. If the dry fish begins to break up, it can be removed half-way through the cooking and returned just before serving. Mix the flour with a tpt of cold water in a small bowl. Add some of the soup slowly, mixing to prevent lumps. Mix the flour and soup mixture into the soup and stir well. Boil for 5 minutes. Cool partially and serve with boiled foods or thickened cassava starch.

Dry Fish and Dry Crayfish Yam Pottage

A complete meal consisting of small lumps of yam in lots of yam-thickened sauce flavoured with dry fish, crayfish and palm oil.

Ingredients	Handy Measure	Metric
Yam	three 3 cm slices, about 12 cm in diameter	500 g
Dry fish	1 medium	250 g
Palm oil	1 tpt or more	70 ml +
Salt	1 dsp	8 g
Onion	½ medium	75 g
Fresh tomato	1 medium	90 g
Fresh red pepper	2 ata rodo and 1 tatasai	
Dry crayfish, small	1 mt	40 g
Dry crayfish (large) or dry oysters, clams or periwinkles	1 mt	50 g

Clean and wash the dry fish well, removing the bones. Grind the tomato, peppers and onions with dry small crayfish. Prepare as simple yam pottage (see Chapter 3), adding whole dry crayfish with heads and tails removed and dry fish with the ground ingredients.

This is a hearty dish which could serve as the main meal of the day. A lightly cooked green vegetable can be folded in just before serving or it can be served as a side dish. It is usually very popular with children.

Thickened Wateryam Soup with Dry Fish

Ijaw: *Ekere fulou*

A simple thickened soup with dry fish and light-textured wateryam.

Ingredients	Handy Measure	Metric
African nutmeg	2 seeds	
Dry ground red pepper	1 dsp	9 g
Fresh palm oil	1 mt	190 ml
Sliced wateryam	8 cm of an 11 cm diameter yam	1.2 kg
Dry fish, dressed	1 medium	225 g
Salt	1 dsp	9 g

Clean the fish. Clean, peel and wash the yam, then cut into 6-8 large pieces. Flame one shelled African nutmeg and grind with the unflamed one. Put the yam in 800 ml (3 mgt) of water, adding the salt and fish. Bring to the boil and cook for 5 minutes. Add the African nutmeg, pepper and oil. When the yam is done, lift the fish out and set aside. Remove 1-2 pieces of yam and mash in a mortar or with some broth in a blender. Return the yam to the soup and stir well until smooth. Place the fish back in the soup and mix gently so as not to break it up.

Dry Fish and Rice Casserole

An economical way of serving rice, particularly popular in the Eastern part of the country. The smoked fish and crisp shrimps are tossed in a palm oil and pepper sauce and cooked with rice.

Ingredients	Handy Measure	Metric
Dry fish, dressed	1 medium	250 g
Palm oil	½ mt	95 ml
Salt	2 tsp	6 g
Onion	½ medium	75 g
Fresh tomato	1 medium	90 g
Fresh red pepper	3 ata rodo or 1 tatasai	
Small dry crayfish	1 mt	40 g
Large dry crayfish	15	
Rice	2 mgt	400 g
Fermented locust beans } optional	1 dsp	10 g
Enge, crushed	1 pod	

Clean the dry fish and remove the bones. Remove the heads and tails from the large dry crayfish and wash the bodies. Wash and pick over the small dry shrimps. Grind the onion, pepper, tomato, small crayfish and fermented locust bean or enge, if used. Crush to crack seeds. Mix all the ingredients except the fish, large dry crayfish, and rice in a large pot (2.5 l). Add water to bring the volume to 600 ml (4 mgt). Add the rice and bring to the boil. Reduce heat to the lowest point, replace the cover and cook over a low heat or in an oven at 250°F, 130°C, until all the water has been absorbed. Allow to 'rest' until partly cooled, on a shelf in the oven with the door ajar.

A complete meal in itself, this dish could be served with a side dish of greens in stew or with a salad.

Dry Fish and Crisp Dry Crayfish in Palm Oil
Yoruba: *Sawa Stew*

A simple oil and dry fish stew with crunchy dry crayfish.

Ingredients	Handy Measure	Metric
Sawa	6 medium	
Dry crayfish (large size)	15	
Onion	½ medium	75 g
Fresh tomato	2 medium	180 g
Fresh pepper	2 ata rodo or 2 tatasai	
Tomato paste	½ tpt	35 g
Salt	to taste	
Palm oil	1 mt	200 ml

Clean the fish (Sawa) and remove the head, tail, skin and large bones, which can be discarded. Break the flesh into small strips (about 1 cm x 3 cm). Clean the crayfish, removing the heads and tails and break the bodies into 2-3 pieces. Grind the heads and tails if they are to be added to the stew. Grind together the onions, pepper and tomato. Place the fish and crayfish pieces in boiling salted water for 5 minutes. Drain and fry the fish and crayfish in heated oil for 5 minutes to give flavour to the oil. Remove fish from oil and set aside. Add ground ingredients, tomato paste and salt to oil. Fry until almost dry: just before the ingredients begin to brown. Add fish, crayfish and ground heads and tails of prawns, if used, and reheat well.

This dish keeps well at room temperature. Traditionally it is carried by farmers and travellers, or given as a gift to an older person who may find regular cooking difficult. Eat with boiled yam or boiled green plantain. It is especially nice eaten with boiled beans and sprinkled with dry white garri. Just before eating, some lightly boiled greens can be added. It can also be eaten with rice, eba, eko, or bread. This dish is served for breakfast, lunch or dinner.

Okro Soup with Dry Fish

A light soup, with a little oil, slightly thickened with okro and flavoured with dry fish and bitter leaves.

Ingredients	Handy Measure	Metric
Okro	10 large or 20 small	150 g
Bitter leaf, prepared	$\frac{1}{2}$ tpt	25 g
Onion	$\frac{1}{2}$ medium	70 g
Fresh tomato	4 medium	350 g
Fresh red pepper	4 ata rodo	
Dry fish, dressed	1 medium	200 g
Palm oil	$\frac{1}{2}$ tpt	35 ml

Grate the okro finely or put in a blender with 1 mgt of water for 30 seconds so that it is finely chopped but not smooth. Prepare the bitter leaves, if fresh (see Chapter 2). Clean the dry fish. Grind the tomato, onion and fresh pepper and boil them in $2\frac{1}{2}$ mgt (500 ml) of water until the pepper is cooked (20 minutes). If the okro has been blended with water, use only 1 mgt of water. Add the bitter leaves, dry fish and palm oil and boil for another 5 minutes. Add the grated okro and cook for 5 minutes, stirring constantly to prevent scorching and boiling over.

This tasty and nutritious yet economical soup is best served with eba or amala, although it can be served with any other thickened or boiled carbohydrate, such as pounded yam, eko, tuwo or fufu. A favourite dish with students.

Dry Fish Agbono Soup with Egusi
Introduced: Satin soup from Sierra Leone

A dry fish soup lightly thickened with a combination of agbono and egusi.

Ingredients	Handy Measure	Metric
Agbono	10 seeds	8 g
Egusi, ground, roasted or unroasted	$\frac{1}{2}$ mt	35 g
Fresh tomato	4 small	200 g
Onion	1 large	150 g
Salt	to taste	
Fresh red pepper	6 ata rodo	
Dry crayfish (small)	1 tpt	15 g
Dry fish	1 medium	250 g
Palm oil	1 mt	200 ml

Grind the agbono or purchase ready-ground. Grind the tomato, onion and fresh pepper together. Clean the dry fish, break into serving-size pieces and soak for a few minutes in boiling water. Grind the egusi or buy pre-ground. Heat the oil, but do not allow it to smoke. Add the agbono and fry lightly (1-2 minutes). Add 2 mgt water (500 ml), ground tomato, pepper, onion and salt to taste. Boil for 15 minutes. Add the ground crayfish, egusi and fish. Boil for a further 5 minutes.

This dish is ideal to eat with fufu, pounded yam, amala, eba or eko. It can also be eaten with rice.

Dry Crayfish Agbono Soup

Ijaw: *Eri otutu fulou*

Tasty crisp dry crayfish in a slightly thickened soup flavoured with agbono, which also gives a slight 'draw' to the consistency.

Ingredients	Handy Measure	Metric
Agbono	1 tpt	50 g
Dry ground red pepper	$\frac{1}{2}$ tsp	1 g
Dry crayfish, large size	1 mgt, dressed	50 g
African nutmeg	2	
Fresh palm oil	1 tpt	70 ml
Salt	1 tsp	3 g
Potash	$\frac{1}{4}$ tsp	1 g
Dry crayfish, small size	1 mgt	50 g

Remove the heads and tails from the large dry crayfish. Grind the heads and tails and the small dry crayfish together. Flame one African nutmeg seed and grind the two seeds together. Mix all the ingredients except the agbono together, adding $1\frac{1}{2}$ mgt (450 ml) water and bring to the boil. Add the ground agbono, stirring constantly to avoid lumps. If lumps form, press them out with the back of a spoon or pour off the soup, leaving the crayfish behind and put into a blender for 30 seconds. Cook, uncovered, for 30 minutes over a medium heat, stirring regularly to prevent scorching or boiling over.

This dish is best cooked in a locally fired clay pot so that the soup cooks down well without scorching. Serve with pounded food. It is especially good with pounded yam and also with eba or fufu. Some people even like it with rice, boiled yam or boiled green plantain.

Simple Agbono and Palm Oil Stew with Dry Fish and Snails

Ingredients	Handy Measure	Metric
Palm oil	1 tpt	70 ml
Potash	$\frac{1}{4}$ tsp	.75 g
Enge	1 pod	
Dry ground red pepper	1 tsp	2 g
Leafy green vegetable	1 mgt	100 g
Dry fish	1 medium	250 g
Snails, dressed	2 medium	100 g
Agbono	1 tpt	25 g
Salt	to taste	

Clean the dry fish well. Dress the snails and boil in 2 mgt of water until tender (about 20 minutes). Drain and add 2 mgt of water, the potash, enge (pounded slightly to crush seeds), pepper, chopped greens, dry fish, palm oil and salt to taste and cook for 5 minutes. Grind the agbono on a stone or in a blender. Mix with a little liquid from the soup to soften it, then blend into the stew, stirring well to eliminate lumps. The dry fish can be lifted out to prevent it breaking up during this stirring process. Simmer for another 5 minutes. Serve with thickened carbohydrate food such as thickened cassava starch or pounded yam.

Dry fish and Egusi Ball Soup
Tiv: *Agbele-chie*

A thick soup with white dumpling-like nutty flavoured egusi balls in a tasty dry fish and greens soup base.

Ingredients	Handy Measure	Metric
Egusi seeds	1½ mgt	200 g
Onion	2 dsp	9 g
Fresh red pepper	2 ata rodo	8 g
Small dry crayfish	½ mgt	35 g
Fermented locust bean	2 dsp	20 g
Dry fish (dressed)	1 medium	100 g
Palm oil	½ tpt	35 ml
Greens (ugu or any other mild but firm leafy vegetable)	10-15 leaves	
Salt	to taste	

Clean the fish and break up into large pieces. Chop onion very finely. Grind egusi or buy ready ground. Clean greens and cut coarsely. Pound the egusi and onion to a smooth paste until the oil oozes out and the solids form a lump. This is best done with a stone, but a mortar is satisfactory. Remove from the mortar and set aside. Pound the pepper, crayfish and locust bean until smooth, using a stone or mortar. Put three-quarters of this paste into a pot containing 3 mgt (800 ml) of water. Mix well, add the dry fish and boil for 10 minutes. Meanwhile, mix the remaining paste with the egusi and onion and form all but 2 tblsp. into irregular-sized balls ½ to 1½ cm in diameter, pressing firmly into shape. Put the remaining 2 tblsp. of the egusi and onion mixture into the stew and stir gently. While the soup is boiling, add the egusi balls and greens. Cover and continue to boil on a medium heat for 15 minutes. Remove cover and cook until the water just covers the egusi balls.

This dish is difficult to prepare, but definitely worth the trouble. It is traditionally served to special guests; the stew is so rich that the egusi balls are sometimes referred to as 'meat'. Traditionally served with pounded yam. Try any other thickened carbohydrate food with it or serve with rice or dodo.

Dry Fish 'Butter'
Ijaw: *Indi ungo*

Well-flavoured dry fish pounded with the best palm oil, potash and spices results in a butter-textured food used as a condiment.

Ingredients	Handy Measure	Metric
Dry fish — well dried variety	1 small	50 g dressed
Dry ground red pepper	½ tsp	1.5 g
Salt	½ tsp	1.5 g
Potash (ground)	½ tsp	3 g
African nutmeg	2 seeds	
Fresh palm oil	1 tpt	70 ml
Boiling water	¾ tpt	50 ml

Clean the dry fish well, removing all the bones and keeping the flesh and skin. Flame one of the African nutmegs and grind the two seeds together in a mortar. Pound the fish in a mortar until it is in small pieces and the skin is well broken up. Add the pepper and African nutmeg, pounding to mix well. Add the oil and potash, pounding to break up the potash well. Add boiling water slowly. It will not separate from the oil as the potash keeps them mixed, but the colour will change from the red-orange of the oil to a bright yellow colour. Scoop into a bowl. As this cools, it will thicken without separating and will take on the consistency of butter, mixed with pieces of fish. Serve within a few hours because it does not store well.

A traditional 'quick food', but a special dish as it requires the best quality ingredients in order to make it delicious. The best oil and the best almost-dry fish are necessary. Serve with boiled green plantain or boiled yam or cocoyam.

Dry Crayfish Pepper Soup
Ijaw: *Eri pouru iginabeni*

A light, unthickened soup without any oil, nicely flavoured with dry smoked shrimps and smoked shrimp eggs.

Ingredients	Handy Measure	Metric
Dry crayfish (large size)	2 mgt	80 g
Salt	1 tsp	3 g
Onion	1 small	75 g
Dry red pepper	1 tsp	2.5 g
Ogougou (smoked dry shrimp eggs)	2 tsp	5 g
Dry fish, optional		

Remove heads and tails from the dry crayfish, Wash the bodies and grind the heads and tails. Put 2 mgt of water in a pot, adding salt, finely sliced onion and red pepper. Boil for 10 minutes. Add dry crayfish, shrimp eggs and ground crayfish heads and tails, together with dry fish if used. Boil for another 10 minutes. Serve with any boiled food, particularly yam or green plantain. Since this is quite rich, a small amount is usually served with a full serving of carbohydrate. Try this pepper soup as an appetizer for a special meal. If dry fish is added to the soup, treat it gently so that it does not break up; serve in large pieces.

Groundnut Stew with Fresh Groundnuts and Dry Fish

Ijaw: *Apapafubu*

Ingredients	Handy Measure	Metric
Fresh or boiled groundnuts	1 mgt	180 g
Fresh tomato	2 medium	180 g
Fresh oil	1 tpt	70 ml
Dry very hot red pepper (*Ikpukpu igina*)	1 tsp	2 g
Fresh or mid-smoked fish	1 medium	250 g
Sliced onion	1 small	75 g
African nutmeg	2 seeds	
Salt	to taste	
Leafy green vegetable, chopped (try *ugu* or *soko*)	1 tpt	25 g

Shell and skin the groundnuts. (If using fresh raw groundnuts, shell, pour boiling water over and remove skins as for beans). Pound in a mortar. Pour the oil into a pot and add salt, onions, ground tomatoes and pepper, and fry for 5 minutes. Add 1 mt of water, vegetables, and fish and cook for 10 minutes. Add pounded groundnuts mixed with a little water. If the fish is fresh or boiled, fry with the other ingredients before the water is added. Boil until the flavours are mixed and the soup is cooked (15 minutes). This stew is best served with fufu, boiled food or rice.

Dry Fish and Cowpea Soup
Yoruba: *Gbegiri*

A rich, tasty cowpea soup with dry fish and dry crayfish. Made with palm oil, it has a pleasant reddish colour.

Ingredients	Handy Measure	Metric
Cowpeas	1½ mt	230 g
Dry fish	1 medium	90 g
Fresh tomato	2 medium	115 g
Groundnut oil or best quality palm oil	1 tpt	50 ml
Dry ground red pepper	1 tsp	1.5 g
Onion	1 small	100 g
Salt	to taste	
Dry crayfish	1 tpt or more	15 g
Okro, optional	½ tpt, chopped	25 g

Soak the cowpeas and remove the husks. Grind the tomatoes and onion. Grind the dry crayfish, either alone or with the tomato and onion. Cook the cowpeas in 6 mt (1.25 litres) of water until soft (about 1 hour). Drain and mash the beans to a coarse texture or sieve. Add water to make a thick or thin soup, depending on how it is to be served. Add all the other ingredients except okro and dry crayfish. Cook on a low heat, taking care not to scorch it, (20 minutes). Add okro and dry crayfish, cook for 3-5 minutes. When thick, this is served with boiled yam or rice. In some places it is also served with okro soup and amala, eba or pounded yam. When thin, it can be used as a soup course in a multi-course meal.

Dry Fish and Sliced Plantain Pottage
Ijaw: *Kekefiai*

A thick creamy pottage with crisp dry crayfish, small pieces of tender green plantain and chunks of dry fish.

Ingredients	Handy Measure	Metric
Green or just ripening plantain	3 medium	700 g
Fresh palm oil or best palm fruit pulp (see Chapter 2)	1 tpt or 2 mgt pulp	
Dry fish (lightly smoked is preferable)	1 medium or 1 large chunk	200 g
Dry crayfish, small size	1 mt	35 g
Dry crayfish, large size	1 mt	35 g
Potash	$\frac{1}{4}$ tsp	.75 g
Salt	1 tsp	3 g
Dry ground red pepper	1 tsp or more	2 g+

Peel and slice the plantain into $\frac{1}{2}$-1 cm slices. Clean the dry fish leaving it in large pieces. Grind the small dry crayfish. Remove the heads and tails from the large crayfish and wash the body. Grind the potash into small pieces. Place the plantain in a pot and put the dry fish on top. Sprinkle on the ground dry crayfish and put the large dry crayfish on top. Add water to cover, then add oil, pepper and salt. Drop the potash in at one side so that it will settle on the bottom and dissolve well. Cover and bring to the boil. Lower the heat, loosen the cover and boil gently until the plantain is soft. Remove the fish and crayfish and stir the soup with a wooden spoon, allowing the softest pieces of plantain to break up, thus thickening the soup, but do not crush the plantain. If preferred, you can take some of the plantain out and mix it in a blender with a little soup, returning it to the pot and mixing gently. Serve the plantain and sauce with the fish and whole crayfish arranged on top.

This is a one-dish meal which it is very easy to eat too much of, as it is rather heavy and rich. Try serving it with a salad, fresh or boiled vegetables, or a tomato salad (see Chapter 7).

Dry Fish and Wateryam Ball Pottage
Yoruba: *Ikokore*

A thick, very rich pottage with a bright red palm oil colour and tender lumps of white wateryam, rather like dumplings in English and American stews.

Ingredients	*Handy Measure*	*Metric*
Wateryam	1 small	1 kg
Palm oil	1 tpt	70 ml
Onion	1 medium	150 g
Fresh tomato	2 medium	180 g
Fresh red pepper	4 ata rodo	
Small crayfish (dry)	1 mgt	50 g
Fresh prawns, optional	1 mgt	300 g
Dried fish: agbodo or oforo (lightly roasted)		100 g dressed
Fermented locust bean, optional	2 dsp	20 g

Grind together the onion, tomato, fresh pepper, crayfish and locust bean, if used. Pick over the dry crayfish and grind separately, if desired. Shell the prawns and wash, if used. Clean the dry fish and break into large pieces. Peel and wash the yam and grate very finely, adding salt to taste. Alternatively, blend small amounts of yam, adding very little water. Put all the ingredients except the yam and lightly roasted dry fish into 3 mgt of water and boil for 15 minutes. Add the dry fish and boil for another 10 minutes. Add the yam gently to the simmering stew in handful-sized lumps. Boil for 10-15 minutes gently and turn without stirring. Most of the yam breaks up to thicken the stew; some lumps remain, which are the 'meat' when protein is in short supply.

Traditionally this is eaten with eba or eko. It is a meal in itself and a very rich one. A small serving with eba or bread and a salad or fresh fruit makes a good meal.

Dry Fish Plantain Pottage
Itsekiri: *Owo*

Large pieces of plantain in a thick spiced sauce with dry fish.

Ingredients	Handy Measure	Metric
Enge	2 pods	
Potash (or ordinary salt)	to taste	
Palm oil	1 tpt	70 ml
Dry, ground red pepper	1 tsp	2 g
Dry fish (lightly smoked is preferable)	1 large chunk or 1 medium whole	200 g
Green plantain	3 medium	700 g
Dry crayfish (large size)	1 tpt	15 g

Wash, clean and salt the dry fish. Grind the dry crayfish heads and tails; wash the bodies. Remove the seeds from the enge and crush in a mortar; use the seeds and hull. Peel the green plantain, cut into thirds and put in a pot. Place the fish on top, add all the other ingredients except the salt and cover with water. Boil down to about three-quarters of the volume, when the plantain should be tender. Remove 2 pieces of plantain and grind with some of the soup in the mortar or a blender. (Cut chunks of plantain into small pieces first not to overwork the motor). Return to the pot, add native salt softened in a teaspoon of warm water and mix well. It can be served alone as a meal or with cooked cassava starch. This is traditionally a special occasion dish. It can also be served with a fresh vegetable such as carrots, or with any salad mixture.

Cowpea Stew with Stockfish

A smooth, thick bean soup with chunks of firm stockfish.

Ingredients	Handy Measure	Metric
Cowpeas	2 mgt	160 g
Bones for stock	2-3 pieces	500 g
Fresh red pepper	6 tatasai or 12 ata rodo	
Onion	1 medium	150 g
Fresh tomato	2 medium	180 g
Stockfish	1 medium	200 g
Fermented locust bean	1 dsp	10 g
Dry, ground red pepper	1 tsp	2 g
Palm oil	½ mt	90 ml
Dry crayfish (small size)	1 tpt	15 g
Salt	to taste	

Break the cowpeas up into small pieces on a stone or with a mortar. Soak the broken cowpeas in twice their volume of water. Cut the stockfish into pieces (this is best done in the market with an electric saw), soak it and boil in water until soft. Wash the bones and place in a pot, add salt and cover with water. Simmer for 1 hour. Remove scum. Grind fresh pepper, onion, tomato and locust beans together. Grind the dry crayfish. Drain the cowpeas and cook in water until the water has evaporated and they are nearly cooked. Add the ground tomato, onion, pepper and locust beans, together with $4\frac{1}{2}$ mgt bone stock. Cook for 10 minutes. Add oil, dry pepper, and stockfish and cook for 15 minutes. Add salt and ground dry crayfish. The soup should now be smooth with all the ingredients evenly mixed. Serve hot with eba. This is good as a side dish with rice and palm oil stew.

Okazi Soup
Ibo: *Okazi Soup*

Yellow-orange soup with firm shreds of okazi greens and chunks of dry fish, flavoured with dry crayfish. The ukpotoro prevents the oil from being 'greasy', and thickens it only slightly.

Ingredients	*Handy Measure*	*Metric*
Dry fish (any type or mixture of types) lightly smoked, very dry, and/or stockfish		200 g
Okazi vegetable, shredded	3 mgt loose shreds	150 g
Palm oil	1 tpt	35 ml
Dry ground red pepper	1 tsp	2 g
Salt	1 tsp	3 g
Ukpotoro seeds or prepared ukpotoro	2 seeds or 3 dsp	25 g
Ground small dry crayfish	1 mgt	50 g

Clean the dry fish and break into large chunks. The amount used is determined by taste and by the money available. One medium dry fish and a small stockfish would make a rich soup. If the stockfish is used, cut in pieces (or have this done in the market) and boil until soft. Shred the okazi vegetable if purchased in leaves. Boil the shelled ukpotoro seeds in a small amount of water for 30 minutes. Pound or grind on a stone until smooth with 1 dsp. of palm oil. Alternatively the ukpotoro may be bought prepared in the market. Grind the dry crayfish. Put the palm oil, dry pepper and 2 mgt (500 ml) water in a pot. Bring to the boil and add the dry fish, ground crayfish and salt. Cook for 15 minutes. Add the ukpotoro and boil for 5 minutes. Add the okazi greens and boil for 5 minutes. This soup is traditionally served with eba.

Prepared Boiled Shrimps
Ijaw: *Puundei Imgbete Meni*

Simply elegant shrimps, lightly salted and peppered.

Ingredients	Handy Measure	Metric
Small fresh shrimps (frozen ones will do)	2 mt	400 g
Onion	$\frac{1}{2}$ small	30 g
Dry red pepper	$\frac{1}{2}$ tsp	1 g
Salt	$\frac{1}{2}$ tsp	1.5 g

Remove the flesh from the washed shrimps. Place the shells, heads, tails, etc. in a mortar and pound with a rubbing motion until the juices are pressed out. Add $\frac{1}{2}$ tpt water and sieve, pressing out the juice and soft material but not letting any shell material through. Grind the onion with a mortar or stone. Mix the sieved pulp, shrimp, water and remaining ingredients together in a pot. Boil until dry, but not burned.

This can either be served alone as a treat or with boiled food as a meal. Try it as an appetizer with toast or fried green plantain (see Chapter 10).

Fresh Roasted Prawns
Ijaw: *Fein Opuru*

Ingredients
Prawns
Salt
Bamboo skewers

Wash the prawns and remove the heads and tails. Place the bamboo skewer through the front and back ends. Salt lightly and place over glowing charcoal, turning occasionally. When well cooked (10 minutes), remove from the heat and serve.

Fresh Roasted Prawns may be served on their own as a snack or with boiled food, soaked garri or farina.

Sautéed Periwinkles and Shrimps

Ingredients	Handy Measure	Metric
Periwinkles, shelled	2 mgt	500 g
Fresh shrimps, small size	1 mgt	300 g
Palm oil (best quality)	½ tpt	35 ml
Salt	to taste	
Garlic	2 cloves, crushed	
Dry ground red pepper	1 tsp	2 g

Clean the periwinkles by removing the soft intestine and hard round 'eye' and shell the shrimps. Heat the palm oil, add the garlic and fry for a minute. Add the shrimps, periwinkles and salt to taste. Fry for 5 minutes. Serve with boiled yam or boiled green plantain.

Fried Shrimps

Ijaw: *Gbaaran opuru*

Shrimps cooked in a fried tomato, pepper and onion palm oil sauce.

Ingredients	Handy Measure	Metric
Shrimps (or prawns)	3 mt	600 g
Fresh palm oil	1 mt	190 ml
Salt	1 tsp	3 g
Onion	1 medium	150 g
Dry ground red pepper	1 tsp	2 g
Fresh tomato	4 medium	360 g

Wash the shrimps, removing heads and tails (if using prawns, shell them). Drain well. Grind the tomato and slice the onion very thinly. Heat the oil, but do not allow it to smoke. Add salt, onion, pepper and tomatoes. Cook until the pepper is well cooked and the sauce is nearly dry (15 minutes or more), taking care that it does not scorch. Add the shrimps and fry until just cooked (about 7 minutes). If using prawns which have been shelled, the cooking time may be shortened.

This is a dish with good keeping quality as there is little water in it. Serve warm with boiled food, particularly boiled green plantain. It is also nice with rice or could be used as a lunch or picnic dish with bread.

Shrimps Steamed in Banana Leaves
Ijaw: *Fina opuru*

Shrimps are lightly mashed with mild spices and wrapped in banana leaves. After steaming, a solid mass of shrimp held together by its own juices results, providing a most tasty and nutritious food.

Ingredients	Handy Measure	Metric
Small shrimps (best if fresh but can be frozen)	$2\frac{1}{2}$ mgt	500 g
Salt	1 tsp	3 g
Dry ground red pepper	$\frac{1}{2}$ tsp	1 g
Onion, optional	2 dsp	18 g
African nutmeg, roasted	2 seeds	
Freshly cut banana or plantain leaves		

Prepare a steamer (see page 43). Wash the shrimps. Remove and reserve the head, tail, shell and legs. Grind the African nutmeg in a mortar or with a stone. Steam the banana leaves for a few minutes over boiling water to wilt them, so they can be folded easily without breaking. Grind the onion, if used. Lightly pound the shrimps in a mortar. Remove to a bowl. Now place heads, tails, etc. in the mortar and pound with a rubbing motion. Sieve with 1 tpt water, allowing the shrimp juice and soft material to go through without any shell. Add this sieved material to the shrimps with salt, pepper, (ground onion if used), and African nutmeg. Taste and adjust spices. Cut the banana leaves and wrap the shrimp mixture either in one large bundle or in several small ones. Tie with string or raffia. Place a few small pieces of banana leaves over the support in the steamer and then place the packets of shrimp on leaves. Cover and steam for 30 minutes; remove cover and continue to steam until the pot is dry. They can be partly cooled and then used, or dried further over a charcoal fire or in the oven. Unwrap and place on a plate to serve.

These are delicious served with boiled foods or on their own as a snack. If kept unwrapped, they can be kept overnight at least and are nice for picnic food. Try them as an appetizer on lettuce leaves.

Shrimp Coconut Rice

Shrimps and rice cooked in rich coconut milk, until the rice grains are soft and separate but not mushy.

Ingredients	Handy Measure	Metric
Coconut	1 medium	800 g
Salt	2 tsp	6 g
Onion	1 small	80 g
Fresh red pepper	1 tatasai or 1 ata rodo	
Shrimps (or prawns), fresh	1½ mgt	450 g
Rice (long grain preferably)	1 mgt	220 g

Shell the shrimps. Prepare the coconut milk (see Chapter 2). Chop the onion and red pepper coarsely. Clean and wash the rice and drain well. Take 2 mgt of coconut milk adding water, if necessary. Add the salt, chopped onion and pepper and bring to the boil in a 1.25 litre pot. Add the rice and shrimps and bring to the boil again. Turn the heat down to the lowest point or place in the oven in a bakeproof dish at 250°F, 130°C. Cook until the liquid is fully absorbed, taking care not to scorch the rice. Mix to loosen the rice grains; replace the cover and allow to 'rest' on a shelf or in the oven with the door ajar for a few hours to improve the blending of the flavours.

Serve Shrimp Coconut Rice with dodo or with roast or fried meat or chicken. It is particularly good with roast pork. A green cooked vegetable dish also goes well when it is the main dish.

Fresh Shrimp and Okro Soup

Ijaw: *Uwo otutu fulou*

Ingredients	Handy Measure	Metric
Okro, $\frac{1}{2}$ sliced and $\frac{1}{2}$ pounded	$1\frac{1}{2}$ mt, total	200 g
African nutmeg, ground	1 seed	
Fresh tomato	1 small	60 g
Dry ground red pepper	$\frac{1}{2}$ tsp	1 g
Best grade palm oil	3 dsp	20 ml
Salt	$\frac{1}{2}$ tsp	1.5 g
Fresh shelled shrimps	1 mt	200 g

Shell and pound the shrimps in a mortar. Put 1 mt of water in a pot and add all the other ingredients. Cook, stirring occasionally to prevent scorching or boiling over, for 5 minutes. Serve with eba, fufu, boiled yam or boiled green plantain.

Shrimp Jollof Rice

Jollof rice of various types is popular throughout Nigeria, particularly for special occasions. The shrimps, ground tomato, onions, pepper and rice are cooked until the grains are soft and separate but never mushy.

Ingredients	Handy Measure	Metric
Shrimps (or prawns), fresh	$1\frac{1}{2}$ mt	500 g
Fresh tomato	4 medium	300 g
Tomato paste	2 dsp	20 g
Onion	$\frac{1}{2}$ medium	75 g
Fresh red pepper	2 ata rodo or 1 tatasai	
Dry ground red pepper	1 tsp	2 g
Groundnut oil	$\frac{1}{2}$ tpt	35 ml
Rice (preferably long grain)	1 mgt	200 g
Salt	3 tsp	9 g

Shell the shrimps. Grind the tomato, peppers, onion and 6-8 shrimps. Wash, clean and drain the rice. Heat the oil until it smokes slightly. Add the ground ingredients and cook for 5 minutes. Add 1 mgt water and tomato paste. Bring to the boil, adding the shrimps, rice and salt; stir. Replace cover and bring to the boil. Turn heat to the lowest point or place in the oven at 250°C, 130°C, in a bakeproof dish. Cook until all the liquid is absorbed completely. Beware of scorching near the end of cooking! Mix to loosen the rice grains, replace the cover and allow to 'rest' on the shelf or in the oven with the door ajar for a few hours to improve the blending of the flavours.

This is usually served with dodo and meat or chicken fried in a stew. It may also be served with a simple shrimp stew and a fresh salad. Store in a refrigerator if kept overnight. It is very tasty on the second day, if reheated in the oven or on the stove, adding a very little water to prevent scorching.

Shrimp Gumbo

Introduced from the southern United States, this is a thin colourful soup without oil. It has large chunks of green okro, fresh red pepper and pink shrimps.

Ingredients	Handy Measure	Metric
Fresh shrimps	1½ mgt	300 g
Okro	2mt, quartered	320 g
Fresh red pepper	1 tatasai or ata rodo	
Dry ground red pepper	to taste	
Onion	1 medium	150 g
Salt	½ tsp	1 g
Fresh tomato	4 medium	350 g
File powder (use bitter leaf)	1 dsp dry or 2 dsp scrubbed and minced	1 g

Shell the shrimps. Cut the okro into quarters. Remove the membranes and seeds of the red pepper and cut into small pieces. Chop the onions into small pieces and grind the fresh tomatoes. Prepare the bitter leaf if used fresh (see Chapter 2). Put all the ingredients in a pot with about 2 mgt of water. Bring to the boil, reduce the heat and simmer for 20 minutes.

This dish is thought to be one carried to the United States from Africa. File powder was probably the replacement for the unavailable bitter leaf. In the United States, this soup is usually served thinner and a small amount of rice added to it ($\frac{1}{2}$ cup cooked rice). For a meal, prepare as described and serve with rice or boiled yam. By cooking the okro with raw onion, the 'draw' is considerably reduced, thus making it more acceptable to American palates, although in many Nigerian dishes 'draw' is desirable.

Marinated Land or Sea Crab
Yoruba: *Imoyo Akan*

A recipe of Brazilian origin, popular among Lagos indigenes. Crab meat and prawns are tossed in a light dressing of olive oil, vinegar, raw tomatoes, onions and fresh pepper.

Ingredients	Handy Measure	Metric
Large land or sea crabs	3	
Vinegar	2 dsp	20 ml
Olive oil or cooked groundnut oil	$\frac{1}{2}$ tpt	35 ml
Dry ground red pepper	1 tsp	2 g
Fresh red pepper	1 ata rodo	
Tomato paste	1 dsp	10 g
Onion	1 small	70 g
Fresh tomatoes	1 medium	90 g
Prawns (or shrimps), fresh	10	
Salt	to taste	

Buy the crabs some days before use and feed them with garri, mixed with palm oil. When ready to use, immerse in boiling water to kill them and then wash well. Cook covered in boiling water for 30 minutes. Drain, cool and reserve the stock. Shell and boil the prawns in a small amount of salted water. Drain and reserve the stock. If groundnut oil is used, heat until it smokes and then cool. Chop the fresh pepper (removing the membranes and seeds), onion and tomato very finely with a knife. Soak the chopped onions, tomatoes and pepper in vinegar and oil. Remove the top shells from the body of the crab and scoop out all the soft dark flesh from inside the top shells into a clean bowl. Discard the stomach attached to the shell below the eyes and the greyish white 'dead man's finger'. Crack the shells, claws and legs. Take out all the white flesh and add to the soft brown flesh. Add 120 ml (1½ tpt) of stock to the crab flesh and then add vinegar, oil, tomato, onion, pepper mixture and tomato paste. Mix well and season with salt.

This is traditionally served with Imoyo Eba, prepared with the crab and prawn stocks. Refrigeration for a few hours helps to bring out the flavours. It may also be served with rice, or as an appetizer heaped on the empty crab shells and accompanied by toast.

6

Land snails

Land snails, although taboo in certain areas, are generally very popular. They are available seasonally in most markets, but are fast becoming a luxury. Land snails are usually sold when they are quite large (300-450 g); small ones are often found by children after the first rains and fried in oil for a treat. Always make sure the snails are alive when bought. They will retreat back into their shells when touched or they will be outside their shells carrying them about. They can be kept alive at home but must be kept very moist and fed, for example, on garri and palm oil. It is a good idea to keep them a few days, as they can then excrete any toxic foods they may have ingested. Keep a weight on the cover of the aerated container or they may escape. In most recipes the shell is discarded, so can be broken when cleaning the snails. Snails can simply be washed in many changes of water to remove the slime or have lime halves or alum rubbed on them to 'cut' the slime. Garri may also be used to 'asborb' the slime. When quite clean, the parts considered edible are saved. You can see this from the diagram below. The snail flesh or 'Congo meat' can be used directly or it can be boiled whole or in pieces and frozen.

Snail recipes

Clean, boiled snails are often added to dishes containing chicken, meat or fish. You will find the recipes in this book. Check the Index for such combinations.

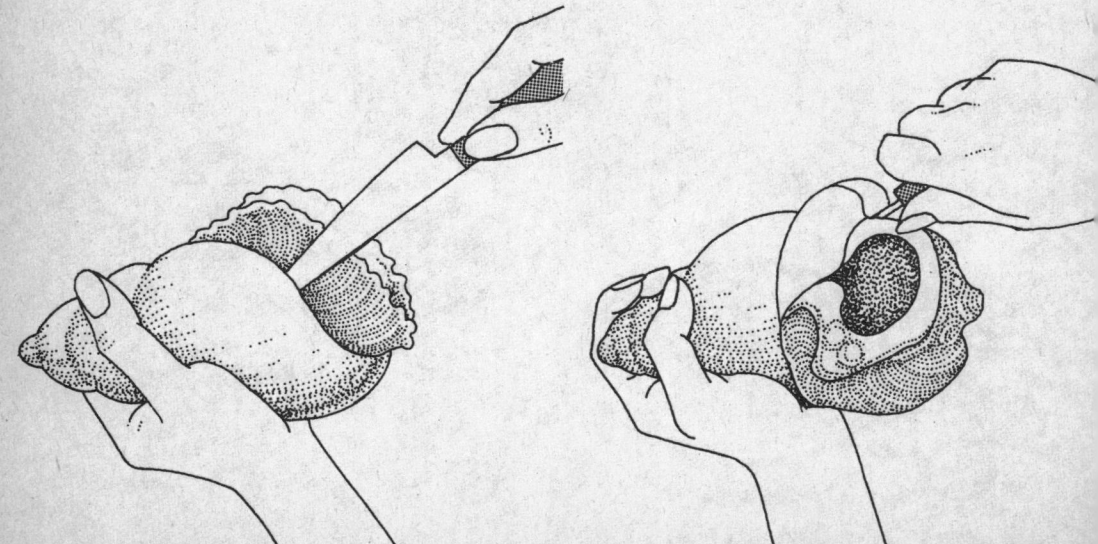

Simple Fried Snails

Buy and feed snails a few days in advance. Crack shells and dress, as shown below. The snails can be parboiled for 3 minutes to remove the remaining slime and fried directly, but even after frying they will be quite tough. If preferred tender, they should be boiled in water to cover until they are pierced easily with a fork. Remove and dry well. Sprinkle liberally with salt and red pepper. Deep fry in oil until partly dry and crisp on the edges. Drain and cut into bite-sized pieces.

Snails Fried in Spicy Sauce

Ingredients	Handy Measure	Metric
Snails, dressed	12 small or 8 large	400 g
Onion	1 medium	150 g
Fresh tomato	2 medium	180 g
Dry ground red pepper	1 tsp	2 g
Salt	to taste	

Boil the snails as above. Grind the tomato and half an onion. Slice remaining onion thinly. Put the oil in a pot and heat until it starts to smoke. Add the ground pepper, tomatoes, onion and salt. Fry for 10 minutes. Add the snails and fry for a further 10 minutes. This dish is popular at parties. It can be served with soaked garri or farina or with a mainly carbohydrate main dish.

Cleaning and Dressing Snails

Snail and Green Plantain Pottage
Ijaw: *Osi fiai*

Whole snails and large pieces of boiled unripe plantain in a simple pottage, thickened with the plantain and coloured with the oil.

Ingredients	Handy Measure	Metric
Green plantain	2-3	600 g
Snails, dressed	6 small	200 g
Salt	1 tsp	3 g
Dry ground red pepper	1 tsp	2 g
Potash	½ tsp	1 g
Palm oil	½ tpt	35 ml

Clean the snails with a brush. Peel the plantain and cut each into 3-4 pieces. Place the plantain and snails in their shells in a pot. Add water to cover. Add palm oil, salt, pepper and potash. When the plantain and snails are soft, remove the snails. Remove the flesh from the shell, cutting away any parts considered inedible. Return the edible portions to the pot and cook for five minutes more. Stir with a wooden spoon so that the plantain thickens the soup. (You can also take 1-2 pieces of plantain, cut into small pieces and blend until smooth in an electric blender with the water from the soup). Serve hot or cold.

Herbed Egusi Soup with Snails and Dry Fish

Ingredients	Handy Measure	Metric
Dry fish, dressed	1 medium	150 g
Snails, dressed	4 medium	150 g
Egusi, roasted or unroasted	1 mgt	140 g
Dry ground red pepper	1 tsp	2 g
Fresh red pepper	2 ata rodo	
Iru	1 dsp	9 g
Dry crayfish	1 mt	40 g
Palm oil	1 tpt	70 ml
Tea-bush leaves	2 mgt, chopped	200 g
Onion, optional	1 tpt chopped	50 g
Salt	to taste	

Clean the dry fish and snails. Cook the snails until tender. Grind the egusi finely on a stone or in a blender. Chop the onion finely, if used, and fry in the oil until soft. Grind the fresh pepper, dry crayfish and iru in a blender with 1 mgt water. Alternatively, grind in a mortar or on a stone and add with the water separately to the fried mixture. Add the chopped tea-bush leaves, fine or coarse according to taste, and the dry fish. Cover and cook for 5 minutes. Add the ground egusi, the snails and salt to taste. Cover and cook, stirring occasionally for 15 minutes. Serve with any thickened carbohydrate food.

Snail Pepper Soup
Ijaw: *Osi Iginibeni*

Whole snails in their shells cooked with large pieces of green plantain in an unthickened soup.

Ingredients	Handy Measure	Metric
Snails	1 dozen small to medium	400 g
Salt	½ tsp	1 g
Dry ground red pepper	1 tsp	2 g
Potash	½ tsp	1 g
Green plantain (may be very green or almost ripe, according to taste)	3 medium	900 g

Clean the snails inside and out after puncturing the membrane covering the opening, if any. Peel the plantain and cut into 2-4 pieces each. Put the snails and plantain in a pot. Just cover with water and add salt, pepper and potash. When the plantain is cooked and the snails are tender, remove from the heat. Place the plantain on one plate and the snails and water on another. When being eaten, snails are extracted with a fork, removing any parts considered inedible in the same way that chicken bones or pork fat are removed when eating them. The bite-sized pieces of plantain are dipped in the water with the snails.

This is a complete meal in itself and would probably only appeal to someone with a real enthusiasm for snails.

Snail Stew
Introduced

Tender chunks of snail flesh in a nicely spiced broth with chopped red tomato and green sweet pepper.

Ingredients	Handy Measure	Metric
Snails, dressed	3 large	200 g
Garlic	1 clove	
Onion	1 medium	150 g
Fresh tomatoes	2 medium	180 g
Green peppers	2 medium	
Fines herbes (or try fresh herbs such as partminger or tea-bush leaves)	1 tsp	
Pepper and salt	to taste	
Butter or groundnut oil	1 tpt	70 ml

Clean the snails and cut the muscle only into large chunks or slices. Chop the tomatoes and green pepper into small pieces. Chop the onion finely. Sauté the garlic in the butter with the sliced snails for 5 minutes. Add the salt, pepper, onion and herbs with water to cover. Simmer until the snails are tender (30-40 minutes). Add the tomato and green pepper and cook for a further 10 minutes. Serve with rice.

7

Vegetables and salads

Green vegetables

There are too many green vegetables used in Nigeria to attempt to list them all. They are important in the diet as they contain vitamins, minerals and often a considerable quantity of plant protein (up to thirty per cent). The use of green vegetables should be increased in most homes. While children here and elsewhere often shun plain cooked leaves, many Nigerian dishes are prepared with other dominant flavours and textures, so that soups with leaves are very acceptable to children, especially if they are allowed to eat them with eba or fufu using their hands! Many of these common green vegetables can be easily grown in small gardens, providing an economical and convenient source of fresh, unprocessed food.

Most Nigerians tend to overcook greens and this, with the practice of cutting them up very finely and draining the water used to blanch them, minimizes their food value. We recommend here the shortest cooking time compatible with digestibility and

Child Eating

usually further suggest that the greens be put directly into the stews, without blanching. All greens are low in calories and thus are good for weight watchers, particularly if they are prepared in foods with little or no oil. The following section lists the most common vegetables and those included in the recipes given here.

Bitter Leaf Bitter leaf is used as a vegetable or herb (see Chapter 2).

Cocoyam Leaves Young cocoyam leaves are used as a vegetable.

Cowpea Leaves Young cowpea leaves are used as a cooked vegetable or in salads.

Cassava Leaves Young cassava leaves are sometimes cooked as a vegetable.

Efo This is a general term of Yoruba origin widely used to refer to any leafy green vegetable used in cooking.

Elephant Grass The succulent shoots of elephant grass are added to stews, providing a texture somewhat like the bamboo shoots used in Chinese cooking.

Ewedu (Yoruba: *Corchorus olitorius*. Common name: crain-crain, shiny-leaf; Ibo: *ahubara*; Efik: *etiyon*) These leaves are used on their own or in soups.

Fluted Pumpkin: *Telfairia occidentalis* (Ibo and others: *ugu*) The young leaves and stems of the fluted pumpkin are used as a popular and expensive vegetable. They do not become soggy when cooked as do some of the other common leaves. They contain twenty-one per cent protein, thirteen per cent oil and many minerals. The seeds of the often huge pumpkins can be boiled, shelled and then eaten like beans, used to thicken soup, or served as nuts for a snack.

Garden Egg Leaves: *Solanum manocarpum* (Yoruba: *efo-osun*; Ibo: *afufu*) There are many varieties of plants related to the egg plant or aubergine. The young leaves are used as a vegetable and the fruits eaten raw or cooked in stews.

Green Beans The young pods of cowpeas or related plants are often added to stews or eaten raw. The Tivs dry them and add them to stews during the dry season when fresh vegetables are scarce. One interesting species used is *Vigna sesquipedalis*, from which pods up to sixty centimetres long can be collected.

Indian Spinach: *Basella alba* This succulent climber is native to India and is becoming more popular in Nigeria as it is easily grown. It is much like the typical spinach of America and Europe.

Okro: *Hibiscus esculentus* (Common name: Lady's fingers) The leaves of this plant are eaten when young, mainly in stews. The plant is mainly cultivated for the young fruit pods, which are usually used fresh, grated to give colour, thickening, and a desired 'draw' to the food. The draw can be cut by cooking with tomato or onion. Okro is also dried and ground for addition to stews. Fresh okro is a good source of plant protein.

Okazi (Ibo): *Gnetum africanum* This is a creeping plant with very firm, dry leaves, which can be stored for long periods. It is expensive, probably because it is seldom cultivated. In some areas, it is believed that if the roots grow under the house, the people within will die. It is usually cut very finely, sometimes followed by pounding to prepare rich vegetable stews. It can be eaten raw in salads.

Green Pawpaw Green pawpaw, like garden eggs and marrow, is sometimes used as a vegetable in soups. The Tivs dry it in thin slices and add it to soups to give texture.

Soko (Yoruba): *Celosia argentea* This is the preferred green in the Western States and is widely available throughout Nigeria. It is used in cooking thick leafy green vegetable stews.

Spinach Like efo, this is a general term for any leafy green vegetable used in Nigerian cooking.

Tea-bush leaves See Herbs, Chapter 2.

Tete (Yoruba): *Celosia viridis* Tete is a close relative to soko and is used interchangeably with it. It is widely available.

Cooking Prawns on a Traditional Stove

Selection of Breads and Cookies

Water leaf: *Talinum triangulare* (Yoruba: *gbure*)   Water leaf is widely consumed in Nigeria, where it is often found as a weed. It can also be easily cultivated. Water leaf contains twenty per cent protein and many vitamins and minerals. It is very succulent and tends to dilute the food when added directly. For this reason, and because it is a bit mucilaginous some people wash the leaves extensively before cooking.

Other vegetables

A wide variety of other vegetables is eaten in Nigeria. Tomatoes of many types are available, firm ripe tomatoes being best for salads. There are several varieties of onions, which can be used interchangeably. The green onion tops and chives are not common, but can usually be found in medicine stalls in any large market. Garlic, as in many other parts of the world, is used as a medicine or a food flavouring. Peppers of many varieties are used as spices and also as thickening, where they are an important source of vegetable nutrients. A wide variety of melons and pumpkins (marrow, squash) is available but they are of limited popularity except in a few locations. It is often the leaves or seeds of the melon or pumpkin which are eaten, rather than the fruit. Other introduced vegetables are cultivated for cash crops and are becoming more popular. These include cabbage, carrots, lettuce and cauliflower (Nigerians often eat the greens, leaving the flower or selling it). While cabbage does not usually 'head' in the southern parts of the country, it is worth cultivating for the young green leaves which can be used in salads or cooked.

Recipes Using Vegetables

Very few vegetables are eaten on their own in Nigeria. They are usually mixed with meat, fish, seeds or carbohydrates. We will include here only those recipes where the green is the main ingredient. Many other recipes containing greens and other vegetables can be found in the Index.

Ewedu Soup

Ingredients	Handy Measure	Metric
Ewedu	5 mgt leaves, pressed into a container	500 g
Fermented locust bean, optional	3 dsp fresh	30 g
Ground red pepper	½ tsp	1 g
Potash	pinch	
Dry crayfish, optional	1 tpt	12 g
Salt	to taste	
Iru	1 dsp	9 g

Wash the ewedu leaves. Bring 2½ mt of water and the potash to the boil, making sure that the potash dissolves. Add very finely chopped ewedu leaves whisking constantly using a local broom or a wire whisk. To facilitate the chopping, use a blender adding a little water. Add the iru, ground dry crayfish, salt and pepper and mix well. Mash the iru with the back of a spoon to break it up. Boil for 5 minutes, stirring to prevent boiling over. Serve with a palm oil stew and amala or eba.

Simple Leafy Green Vegetable Stew

Ingredients	Handy Measure	Metric
Leafy green vegetable soko, tete, ugu etc.)	4 bundles	600 g
Fresh pepper	6 ata rodo or 3 tatasai	
Onion	1 medium	150 g
Fresh tomato	3 medium	270 g
Fermented locust bean, optional	1 dsp	10 g
Dry crayfish	1 mt	40 g
Cooking oil (palm, groundnut or vegetable)	½ mt	90 ml
Salt	to taste	

Cut the leaves from the large main stem and wash thoroughly. Grind the onion, tomato, fresh pepper and locust bean, if used, and fry in the oil for 5 minutes. Add ½ tpt water and the coarsely chopped greens. Cover and steam for 5 minutes. Add the ground dry crayfish and season with salt and dry pepper to taste.

Note: The leaves can be added whole and chopped in the stew with two knives after cooking. Serve with eko, eba or other similar food, or rice, and a protein-containing dish (try a simple palm oil stew with meat or fish, or simply fried meat or fish).

Bitter Leaf Stew with Meat and Stockfish
Ibo: *Ofe Onugbu*

Ingredients	Handy Measure	Metric
Stockfish	1 small	200 g
Beef, boiled or dried	1 mgt	160 g
Dry fish, cleaned	1 medium	250 g
Salt	1½ tsp	4 g
Dry crayfish	2 mt	70 g
Cocoyam, grated	1 mgt	200 g
Palm oil	1 tpt	70 ml
Fermented locust bean, mashed	1 dsp.	10 g
Potash, ground	1 tsp.	3 g
Dry ground red pepper	2 tsp.	4 g
Bitter leaves	1 bunch	200 g
Stock cubes, optional	2	

The quantities of stockfish, meat and/or dry fish are not absolute; use as available. Boil the stockfish in water with or without stock cubes until tender (1 hour). Wilt the leaves and small stems of the bitter leaf overnight and then wash well (without chopping) to remove some of the bitterness. Place 2 mt of stock from beef or fish in a pot with the potash, pepper, locust beans, salt and ground dry crayfish. Boil for 5 minutes. Add the cocoyam, meat, dry fish and stockfish. Cover tightly and cook for 10 minutes. The cocoyam will thicken the stew. Add the bitter leaf; cover again and steam for 20 minutes, stirring occasionally to prevent scorching. Serve in a locally made clay pot with cassava fufu or other thickened carbohydrate food.

Simple Greens and Egusi Soup

Ingredients	Handy Measure	Metric
Water leaves, packed	2 mgt	200 g
Egusi seeds	½ mt	50 g
Dry ground red pepper	1 tsp	2 g
Fermented locust bean, optional	1 dsp	10 g
Onion	1 medium	150 g
Good palm oil	½ mt	90 ml
Dry crayfish, ground, loose	1 tpt	10 g
Fresh tomato	2 small	120 g

Wash the water leaves thoroughly. Grind the onion, tomato and locust bean, if used, until smooth. Grind the egusi seeds until fine but not smooth. Fry the ground ingredients in the oil for 5 minutes. Add ½ mt of water, cover and steam for 5 minutes. Add the finely chopped water leaves, cover and steam for 5 minutes. Add the ground dry crayfish, salt and pepper to taste and heat thoroughly. Serve with eba or pounded yam, rice or a boiled carbohydrate vegetable, and with protein food such as a palm oil stew with fish, meat, innards or cow foot.

Boiled Grated Okro

Chop the okro finely with a knife or grate finely using a grater used for coconut. Okro can be put in a blender, although this is not always successful as it purées some seeds and leaves some pods whole, due to the thick mucin in it. If it is blended in small amounts with a lot of water, the product may be acceptable. If the okro is frozen, it can be grated most conveniently when partially thawed. The amount of water added to the okro depends on taste. Try adding equal quantities of water and grated okro, then add more water if desired. Boil the water to be used, and dissolve a pinch of potash in it. Then add 2 dsp. of dry ground crayfish and/or 4 dsp. iru, if desired. Add okro and salt to taste. Boil for 5-10 minutes, stirring well to prevent it from boiling over. Serve with a palm oil stew containing fish, meat or chicken and eba, pounded yam or eko.

Quick Okro and Locust Bean Stew
Tiv

Ingredients	Handy Measure	Metric
Whole dry small peppers	10-15	150 g
Fermented locust bean	3 dsp	30 g
Small tender okro	20	150 g

Pound the locust bean and pepper until smooth. Boil the okro until soft (10 minutes) and then drain. Add the okro to the locust bean and pepper in the mortar. Add salt to taste and mix well. Serve immediately with a thickened carbohydrate food.

Curried Okro
Introduced

Ingredients	Handy Measure	Metric
Onion	2 large	300 g
Vegetable oil or ghee	3/4 mt	170 g
Garlic	4 cloves	
Black pepper	pinch	
Salt	½ tsp	1.5 g
Curry powder	1 dsp	9 g
Fresh tomato	2 small	120 g
Tea-bush leaves ⎫ optional	4-6 leaves	
Coriander powder ⎭	2 tsp	4 g
Turmeric, dry	½ tsp	1 g
Okro	25 large	450 g

Slice one onion and fry in oil. Purée the other onion, tomato and garlic in a mortar or blender. Add to the onions with the remaining spices. Cook on a medium heat for 5 minutes. Cut the heads and tails off the okro and cut into 2-3 pieces each. Add to the spices and cook over a low flame for 10-15 minutes until the okro is tender but retains its shape. Serve with rice and a soup or stew containing meat, such as chicken.

Salads

Traditionally vegetables are not eaten raw in Nigeria. However, salads are becoming increasingly acceptable and are often served at parties, as an accompaniment to traditional dishes. Since raw vegetables retain more vitamins than cooked ones, this is a good trend. It is important to make sure that all raw vegetables are not only thoroughly washed, but also sterilized to kill parasites and other micro-organisms which can cause serious illnesses.

Sterilizing in boiling water (blanching) may be effective, but it destroys the looks and texture of vegetables to be eaten raw. Some individuals soak vegetables in a strong salt solution and/or rub the vegetables in salt. This is effective if done carefully but it often is not. The most reliable method is soaking in a dilute solution of Milton for 15 minutes. The leaves and vegetables should be loosely placed in the Milton solution and rinsed well after draining in clean (boiled and cooled if tap water is not drinkable) water.

The salads given here are some we have found to be well received by many Nigerians. There are many other ways to serve raw fruits and vegetables.

Oil Bean Salad

Ibo: *Ugbakala*

Ingredients
Prepared oil bean
Finely sliced okazi leaves
Finely sliced garden egg (small yellow variety preferred)
Palm oil
Potash

Soften $\frac{1}{2}$ tsp. potash in 1 tsp. of warm water. Stir in a tpt. warm palm oil and mix until thickened. Stir in the salt and ground dry red pepper to taste. Place equal parts of sliced oil bean, okazi and garden egg in mounds on a plate. Serve with prepared palm oil as dressing.
This food is served traditionally at important ceremonial gatherings with cola nuts and palm wine.

 ## Tomato Salad I
Introduced from India

Ingredients	Handy Measure	Metric
Fresh ginger, chopped	3 dsp	25 g
Onion	1 small	100 g
Lemon juice	4 dsp	36 ml
Salt	1½ tsp	4 g
Fresh tomato	4 medium	360 g
Olive oil or vegetable oil	3 dsp	25 ml
Vinegar	2 dsp	18 ml
Sugar	1 tsp	3 g

Mash the succulent outer parts of the ginger root with the back of a spoon or slice it finely. Cut the onion into very thin slices or chop finely. Cut the tomatoes into quarters, if small, or 2 cm chunks if large. Mix all the ingredients gently. Chill and serve.

Traditional Hospitality

Tomato Salad II

Ingredients	Handy Measure	Metric
Fresh tomato	4 medium	360 g
Onion	1 small	100 g
Vegetable oil	3 dsp	25 ml
Vinegar or lemon juice	3 dsp	25 ml
Salt and pepper	to taste	
Chopped partminger leaves	a handful	

Slice the tomatoes and arrange on a serving dish. Sprinkle with finely chopped onion. Blend the vinegar, salt and pepper and then add oil. Pour this dressing over the tomato and onion and sprinkle with partminger leaves.

Cucumber Salad

Introduced from India

Ingredients	Handy Measure	Metric
Cucumber	1 medium	
Yoghurt	1 mt	200 g
Salt	$\frac{1}{2}$ tsp	1 g
Dry ground red pepper	to taste	
Mint or partminger	a few leaves	

Chop the cucumber (peeled or unpeeled and sterilized) coarsely. Mix with the yoghurt and salt. Sprinkle with red pepper and chopped leaves. Chill and serve.

Cooked Salad Dressing

This is a good substitute for mayonnaise. It is made from readily available ingredients and can be kept refrigerated for up to two weeks. Real mayonnaise should only be made from eggs of assured health standards and even so does not keep well. This recipe requires the use of a blender.

Ingredients	Handy Measure	Metric
Flour	½ mt	60 g
Water	1 mt	190 ml
Vinegar or lemon juice	1 tpt	70 ml
Salt	1½ tsp	4 g
Dry mustard, optional	1½ tsp	3 g
Black pepper, ground, optional	1 tsp	2 g
Vegetable oil	1 mt	190 ml
Eggs, large	2	

Boil the flour, water, salt, pepper, dry mustard and vinegar for 1 minute. Put the eggs in the blender and add the cooked paste. Blend for 1 minute. Then add the oil, slowly until it is homogenized and the product is creamy and smooth. Use with any raw or cooked vegetable salad. It is very nice with tossed lettuce, tomato, and avocado pear salad.

Note: The consistency of the chilled dressing will depend on the particular vegetable oil used. Some oils give an undesirably firm dressing but these can be used after bringing to room temperature or can be thinned with vinegar or milk.

Cole Slaw
Introduced

Ingredients	Handy Measure	Metric
Grated or sliced cabbage	3 mt	600 g
Grated carrot	1 mt	200 g
Green sweet pepper or tatasai	1	
Sugar	1 tsp	3 g
Black pepper	¼ tsp	.75 g
Salt	½ tsp	1 g
Vinegar	1 dsp	9 ml
Mayonnaise or substitute	½ mt	90 g
Grated garlic, optional	1 clove	

Remove the membranes and seeds from the pepper and chop finely. Mix fresh pepper, cabbage and carrot. Mix the remaining ingredients and pour over the vegetables. Toss well and chill. Serve on lettuce leaves.

Avocado Pear Salad

Avocado pears make nice additions to salads. They should be peeled and added just before use as they discolour on standing. They keep their colour longer if the peeled fruit is dipped in lemon juice. Try serving halved with salt or filled with any of the salads in this chapter. Fresh shelled and boiled shrimps may be blended with any salad dressing and red pepper to fill the halved avocados for individual servings at a formal dinner.

8

Simple soups, stews and sauces

In this section we have included some soups, stews and sauces which are not complete meals or do not have one main ingredient, so that they do not fit in elsewhere. The majority of these would be served with a carbohydrate for a light meal, while others would be served as an accompaniment to a mainly protein dish (meat, fish or egg). Some traditional soups and other introduced soups, such as the coconut soups, would be excellent appetizer soups for the first course of formal meals.

Simple Palm Oil or Groundnut Oil Stew I

Ingredients	Handy Measure	Metric
Fresh red pepper (tatasai and/or ata rodo)	1 mt, chopped	200 g
Onion	1 large	250 g
Dry ground red pepper	to taste	
Fresh tomato	2 medium	180 g
Palm oil or groundnut oil	1½ mt	300 ml
Dry crayfish, ground, loosely packed	1 tpt	20 g
Salt	to taste	

Remove the heads and tails from the crayfish and grind. Grind the pepper, onion and tomatoes, using as little water as possible. Heat the oil until it just starts to smoke. Fry the ground ingredients for 5 minutes or until nearly all the water has evaporated and small bubbles cover the surface of the oil. Add the ground crayfish parts and whole crayfish, and cook for another minute. If preferred, all the crayfish may be ground. This is a basic stew to which cooked or dried meat, fish, poultry, snails, leafy vegetables etc. can be added. It may also be used as ketchup to add zest to carbohydrate vegetables or meats.

Simple Palm Oil Stew II

Ingredients	Handy Measure	Metric
Dry crayfish	1 tpt	10 g
Salt	to taste	
Palm oil	1 tpt	70 ml
Potash	a pinch	

Grind the dry crayfish and put with the potash, salt and pepper in a small amount of water (1 tpt). Boil uncovered for 5 minutes. Add the palm oil slowly and cook uncovered until most of the water has boiled off. Serve with boiled plantain or yam. This is more like a sauce and is served as a condiment.

Millet Soup

Ingredients	Handy Measure	Metric
Dry fish or crayfish, ground	1 tpt	20 g
Millet flour	1 mt	150 g
Fresh tomato	2 medium	180 g
Onion	2 medium	300 g
Salt	to taste	
Dry ground red pepper	to taste	

To 6 mt of water, add ground tomato, onion and dry fish and bring to the boil. Add the millet flour and seasonings and stir until smooth and thickened. Simmer for 30 minutes.

Cowpea Flour Soup

Ingredients	Handy Measure	Metric
Cowpea flour	1 mt	115 g
Dry fish	1 small	120 g
Cooking oil		50 ml
Stock cubes	2	
Fresh tomato	1 large	115 g
Onion	1 small	75 g
Dry ground red pepper	½ tsp	1 g
Salt	1 tsp	1 g
Water	7 mt	1.3 l

In a large pot, fry the ground tomato, onion and pepper in oil for 5 minutes. Add the stock cubes and water. Blend the cowpea flour with a little water and add to the soup, stirring briskly to prevent lumps. Cook for 30 minutes until the beany flavour disappears, adding salt and pepper to taste. Clean the dry fish and break into small chunks. Add to the mixture in the pot and cook for 10 minutes more. Serve.

Variations Add 1 dsp. fermented locust bean ground with tomato and onion. Add some finely chopped leafy vegetable with the fish. Serve with garri, fufu or tuwo or as an appetizer soup.

Simple Quick Pepper Soup

Ingredients	Handy Measure	Metric
Chicken or beef stock cubes	4	
Cooked goat, beef or chicken in small pieces	1 tpt	80 g
Well-flavoured dry fish in small pieces	1 tpt	60 g
Dry crayfish, ground	2 dsp	18 g
Dry ground red pepper	½ tsp	1 g
Tea-bush leaves, chopped	2 dsp	15 g

Simmer all the ingredients together for 10 minutes. Serve with a boiled carbohydrate vegetable for a light supper or with sandwiches and a salad.

Simple Agbono Soup

Ingredients	Handy Measure	Metric
Agbono	½ tpt	12 g
Fermented locust bean	1 dsp.	9 g
Dry ground red pepper	1 tsp.	1 g
Fresh tomato, ground	2 medium	180 g
Tomato paste	1 dsp.	10 g
Stock (from meat or fish) or stock cube	1 mt	190 ml
Dry fish, cleaned or dry crayfish	1 tpt	30 g
Salt	to taste	

Remove the skin of the agbono by scraping with a knife. Grind the seeds. Heat the oil and melt the agbono in it. Heat the stock and add the melted agbono. When the stew bubbles, add the other ingredients except the fish or crayfish. Allow to cook for 7-10 minutes, stirring constantly. Wash and flake the fish if used and add the fish or ground crayfish. Heat well for two minutes, stirring to prevent it from boiling over or sticking to the bottom of the pan. Serve separately in a bowl as an accompaniment to stew with meat or fish. It may also be served with eba, amala or other thickened carbohydrate foods.

Uncooked Fried Agbono Soup
Ijaw: *Ikiri-igina*

Ingredients	Handy Measure	Metric
Ground agbono seeds, loosely packed	½ mgt	100 g
Large dry crayfish, small dry crayfish and/or dry fish	1 mgt	50 g
Whole dry red peppers	2 tsp	4 g
African nutmeg, roasted	2 seeds	
Salt	to taste	

Pound the peppers coarsely. Pound the crayfish coarsely, having removed the heads and tails. Alternatively, if fish is used, pound coarsely. Fry the ground agbono in a dry skillet, stirring constantly until dark brown. Pound the African nutmeg until smooth. Put the crayfish or fish into a mortar and add the agbono, pepper and African nutmeg, one at a time, pounding between each addition. Then add boiling water a little at a time, pounding continuously until a soup of light dropping consistency is achieved (about $1\frac{1}{2}$ mgt water). Add salt to taste. Eat immediately with boiled green plantain, wateryam, eba or fufu.

Simple Herb Sauce
Igalla dish

Ingredients	Handy Measure	Metric
Tea-bush leaves	2 mt, pressed	135 g
Good palm oil	½ tpt	35 ml
Salt	½ tsp	1½ g
Dry ground red pepper	1 tsp	1 g

Pound or blend the leaves into a paste with as little water as possible. Heat the palm oil, salt and pepper to taste. Add the leaf paste and heat through. Serve with boiled yam. It is also good with fried meat, snails or fish.

Simple Okro Soup

Ingredients	Handy Measure	Metric
Okro	30 medium	300 g
Fermented locust bean	1 dsp	10 g
Oil (groundnut or palm)	4 dsp	35 ml
Large fresh peppers	8 ata rodo	
Dry ground crayfish	2 dsp	5 g
Water or stock	2 mgt	550 ml
Potash	pinch	

Grind the locust bean and pepper. Wash the okro thoroughly and cut up finely. Mix the ground ingredients, palm oil and potash softened in 1 tsp. of warm water. Cook for 5 minutes. Add the stock and okro and boil for 5 minutes. Finally, add the crayfish and cook for 2 minutes. Serve hot with amala, eko or fufu.
Variation 200 g cooked dry or boiled meat in chunks can be added at any time during the cooking.

Prepared Pepper
Ijaw: *Tau igina*

Ingredients	Handy Measure	Metric
Fresh pepper	1 ata wewe	
Fresh pepper	1 ata rodo	
Onion	2 dsp chopped	18 g
African nutmeg, roasted	2 seeds	
Dry or partly dried fish (very good quality)	1 small, dressed	40 g
Salt	to taste	

Pound the peppers in a mortar. Add the onion and pound until fine. Add the African nutmeg and pound again until fine. Then add the flaked fish and salt to taste. Pound for a few minutes to mix the ingredients well. Serve immediately with boiled cocoyam or boiled green plantain. Prepared Pepper is used more as a relish than a stew.

Fruit, Vegetables and Spices

Puff-puff and Chin-chin

Peppered Oil Sauce I
Introduced from Ghana

Ingredients	Handy Measure	Metric
Dry crayfish	1 mt	40 g
Dry whole pepper	1 mt	40 g
Groundnut oil or palm oil	1 squash bottle	750 ml
Salt	to taste	

Grind the dry crayfish and pepper. Put all the ingredients into a cooking pot, place on the fire and fry until all the water has evaporated. Store in a clean bottle. Use as a sauce like ketchup.

Peppered Oil Sauce II

Ingredients	Handy Measure	Metric
Dry crayfish	1 mt	40 g
Fresh pepper, whole	2 mt	80 g
Onion, finely chopped	1 small	75 g
Groundnut oil or palm oil	1 squash bottle	750 ml
Salt	to taste	

Prepare in the same way as Peppered Oil Sauce I above.

'Nigerianised' Packet Soups

Commercially prepared dry soups in packets are often purchased because they are simple to prepare and can be stored for emergency use. They are also, indefensibly, commonly used in restaurants. These soups can be improved by the addition of local foods and spices, as suggested below.

If the soup contains noodles or is a clear type, additions can be made before or after cooking. If it is a cream soup (less desirable), they are best made after bringing the soup to the boil, as all the lumps should be removed before adding the other ingredients.

To 850 ml of soup, add one or more of the following:
2 dsp dry ground crayfish

1 tpt large or small dry crayfish (heads and tails removed)
2 dsp chopped tea-bush leaves or partminger
dry ground red pepper to taste
1 tpt small pieces cooked goat, chicken, beef or dry fish and dry pepper

Laitan's Coconut Soup

Ingredients	Handy Measure	Metric
Flour	2 mt	250 g
Margarine or butter	$\frac{1}{2}$ packet or $\frac{1}{2}$ mt	100 g
Milk (evaporated)	1 small tin	190 ml
White pepper	1 tsp	2 g
Coconuts	4 medium	3 kg
Salt	to taste	

Prepare the coconut milk from the coconuts (see Chapter 2) using 6 cups of hot water. Heat the margarine until melted and blend in the flour. Add the coconut milk and evaporated milk, slowly at first to prevent the formation of lumps. Bring to the boil, adding salt and pepper to taste. Serve very hot immediately.

Coconut Curry Soup

Ingredients	Handy Measure	Metric
Coconut	1 medium	800 g
Milk	as required	
Commercial cornflour (cornstarch)	2 dsp	18 g
Curry powder	1 tsp	2 g
Salt	1 tsp	3 g
Chicken broth or chicken stock cube in water	1 mt	200 ml

Prepare the coconut milk (see Chapter 2) and make up to 3 mgt with milk if necessary. Mix the cornflour with a little milk to form a paste. Boil all the ingredients except the paste. Then add the paste, stirring constantly, until the soup is thickened. Serve hot, garnished with yoghurt.

9

Milk, cheese and eggs

Most milk, cheese and egg dishes are, in a sense, introduced foods. Traditionally, chickens were not raised for eggs. When eggs were available, they were not often given to children as it was widely believed that they would encourage them to become thieves. Fortunately, eggs are now readily available and are an important source of protein for all ages. Guinea fowl eggs are widely believed to be more nutritious than chicken eggs but there is no scientific basis for this. The shells are harder and therefore the eggs easier to transport. Boiled guinea fowl eggs are often hawked at motor parks, to be purchased by travellers.

Eggs can be served at any meal of the day. An almost unlimited variety of foods can accompany them or be folded into them. The addition of eggs is an excellent means of adding extra protein to a meal. Eggs are more easily digested when cooked slowly over a low heat, although most Nigerians prefer them very well done.

Fresh cow's milk is not generally taken, with two exceptions. Fresh and fermented milk (rather like yoghurt), is taken, alone and with cereal porridges among the cattle raising people of the North. Secondly, in some areas of Nigeria, a fresh milk curd cheese called wara is made for local consumption. Wara is somewhat like cream cheese in texture with a mild flavour. The curdling process is produced by the addition of a ground herb, *Calotropis procera*, bits of which can be found in the final product, giving it a pleasant taste. It is safe eaten directly, although it is often lightly fried in chunks in a simple palm oil stew. Wara is not, however, widely available presumably because milking cows are not widespread. Perhaps, in the future, goat's milk will be an acceptable alternative as goats are found everywhere. Wider use of wara should be encouraged, particularly for children.

Fresh milk is available from government experimental farms in a few places. It should always be boiled to ensure that it is free of pathogenic micro-organisms. It is generally very rich and creamy. Imported milk is available in a variety of forms. There are many 'baby milks' or formulae of dehydrated cow's milk and other vitamin and mineral supplements. Other dehydrated whole milks are often fortified with vitamins A and D, and are usually instant mixes. Dry skimmed milk is seldom seen. 'Tinned milk' in Nigeria means evaporated milk in cans. This milk, reconstituted with an equal quantity of water, can be used as cow's milk. Sweetened condensed milk is sometimes available. This is evaporated milk to which a large quantity of sugar has been added. It is often used as a spread on bread or in hot beverages. Milk is used most commonly in beverages such as coffee, tea and chocolate and with thickened starch such as ogi and custard from maize.

Fried Eggs

Break the eggs into a bowl, taking care not to break the yolks. Spread 1-3 dessertspoons palm oil or other cooking oil over the bottom of a heavy skillet (frying pan). Heat until the oil just begins to smoke. Turn off the heat. Immediately add the eggs and cover tightly. The heat from the pan will cook the eggs in 3-4 minutes, setting the yolks only slightly. If you want the yolk very hard, turn the heat on low for a few minutes. For digestibility, do not over-heat or over-fry.

Nigerian Fried Eggs

Ingredients	Handy Measure	Metric
Eggs (try guinea fowl eggs)	4	
Groundnut oil	$\frac{1}{2}$ mt	100 ml
Onion	$\frac{1}{2}$ medium	75 g
Fresh tomato	2 medium	180 g
Fresh red pepper	6 ata rodo or	25 g
	3 tatasai	75 g
Salt	to taste	

Heat the oil until it is almost smoking and turn off the heat. Add the eggs gently to prevent breaking the yolks. Cook until completely set, reheating only if necessary. Remove the eggs from the oil. Fry the coarsely chopped or ground onion, tomato and red pepper in the oil for 5 minutes. Drain off the excess oil. Salt the remaining mixture to taste and place on the eggs. Serve with boiled yam or bread.

Scrambled Eggs

Beat the eggs with a fork and add salt and pepper to taste. Evaporated milk, up to 2 dsp. per egg, may be added (if desired). Put 1 tsp. oil or butter on the bottom of a thick frying pan and heat but do not allow to smoke. Add the eggs, stirring gently as they thicken. When thickened completely, remove from the pan and serve. Try serving with some left-over stew (palm oil stews, egusi soup etc.) for breakfast or a light meal.

Boiled Eggs

Put sufficient water to immerse the eggs in a pot and bring to the boil. Reduce the heat to very low and add the eggs at room temperature. For soft-boiled eggs, remove the eggs after 2-3 minutes. For medium soft eggs, remove the eggs after 4 minutes. For hard-boiled eggs, remove the eggs after 15 minutes. When you remove the hard-boiled eggs from the fire, immerse immediately in cold water to stop the cooking process and to prevent discolouration of yolks. Very fresh eggs are more difficult to shell than eggs which are a few days old.

Omelette

To prepare an omelette, you 'simply' mix an egg well, and fry it in oil. Yet there are entire books devoted to just this one dish. Each country seems to have its own special way of preparing an omelette. A few ways easily adapted to Nigerian foods are suggested here. Serve omelettes with any boiled carbohydrate food or bread.

The first type of omelette is prepared by cooking the eggs separately from the other ingredients. The second type of omelette is prepared by adding the other ingredients to the eggs before they are cooked.

I Mix four eggs, with a fork, until well blended. Add salt to taste ($\frac{1}{4}$ tsp. or less). Cover the bottom of a heavy skillet with $\frac{1}{2}$ tsp. to 3 dsp. of oil, depending on taste. Heat the oil until it just begins to smoke. Add the egg and turn the heat down to lowest point. When well set on the bottom, turn over in one piece, turn off heat and allow to set well. Remove to a serving dish and cover with any of the following ingredients. These ingredients can also be sprinkled over the egg before turning it over in the skillet.

Additions Use one or more of the following: dry crayfish (heads and tails removed soaked in hot water for 5 minutes; chopped green pepper or tatasai (raw or fried lightly in oil); sardines; whole or broken cooked fish; chopped meat; chicken or shrimp; onion (raw or fried); sliced tomatoes; raw or fried; corned beef; chopped tea-bush or partminger leaves; black pepper; a few dessertspoons of remaining palm oil stew.

Try frying these additions lightly in ½ mt oil and then pour on the mixed eggs, lower the heat and cook until partly set. Turn eggs over and cook until completely set.

II   Mix four eggs, with a fork, until well mixed. Add salt to taste. Cover the bottom of a heavy skillet with ½ tpt. oil and heat until it just begins to smoke. Fold in any of the ingredients suggested for Omelette I. Fry on low heat, turning when set on the bottom.

Madras Egg Curry
Moote Kari (introduced)

Ingredients	Handy Measure	Metric
Onion, chopped	1 tpt	50 g
Garlic, minced	4 cloves	
Vegetable oil	2 dsp	18 ml
Curry powder	2 tsp	4 g
Tomato paste	2 dsp	18 g
Water	¾ mt	140 ml
Salt	1 tsp	1 g
Lemon juice	1 tsp	3 ml
Hard-boiled eggs	6	

Sauté the onion and garlic in oil with the curry powder for 3-4 minutes. Add tomato paste and water then cook for 3-4 minutes. Add salt and lemon juice. Stir and cook for about 1 minute. Add halved eggs, heat through and serve with rice.

Yoghurt

Ingredients
Yoghurt starter
Milk

Any type of milk can be used for yoghurt. The best flavour is obtained from fresh cow's milk. Reconstituted dried milk is also good if carefully prepared. Reconstitute dried milk as recommended by the manufacturer for whole milk. Bring the fresh reconstituted milk to the boil (a thick aluminium pan is best), watching carefully to avoid scorching or boiling over. Remove from heat, cover, and cool to 110°F, 43°C. Remove the scum, stir and add 1 tsp. yoghurt. This is the starter. Stir once and cover. The yoghurt culture must now be incubated in a warm place free from draughts, where it will not be disturbed for several hours. Put 2 mt cold water with $\frac{1}{2}$ mt boiling water in a large metal or enamel pan. Then lower the container of milk and starter into the water, being sure the water does not reach the edge of the yoghurt container. Cover with a lid and a thick towel. Place in a cold oven or on top of a cupboard and leave for 5-8 hours, depending on the quantity and room temperature. Chill and use. Keep in a refrigerator for 3-4 days. The yoghurt is ready when it is 'set', that is when it is no longer liquid. Yoghurt for the starter can be obtained from commercial sources, although this is frequently unsuccessful, or from friends, particularly those from Asia, who make it every day.

If one is careful to keep all the materials used in making yoghurt meticulously clean and allow the milk to come fully to the boil, it should be possible to continue making yoghurt indefinitely. In practice, however, yoghurt making may be unsuccessful or interrupted for many reasons. A starter can be kept for long periods by freezing some good yoghurt in a small container. This yoghurt can be removed and used as starter when needed, though it may require a longer time to 'set' at first.

Miriam likes thick yoghurt which looks and tastes like cultured sour cream. For this, use twice the amount of dry whole milk powder. Thus for instant mixing powders, half a cup of dry milk would be dissolved in $1\frac{1}{2}$ cups of warm water and boiled.

Try using thick yoghurt in the following ways:
Use as a salad dressing, salted with the addition of fresh herbs or chopped raw onion to taste.
Mix an equal quantity with boiled salad dressing (see Chapter 8). Add chopped herbs or onion to taste.
Serve alone in a separate bowl with fruits and fruit salads.
Mix 2 dsp. honey into a mgt of yoghurt and serve with fruit salad or sliced pawpaw or pineapple.
Serve alone as a dessert sprinkled with brown sugar.
As a light lunch, serve a mgt yoghurt mixed with 1 tpt chopped fruit. For example, scoop the orange flesh out of halved fruits, chop or mash a ripe banana or chop a pineapple.

10

Small chop, snacks and beverages

Many foods are eaten traditionally as snacks and as light meals during working hours in urban areas. A selection of these and other foods suitable for parties and picnics is included here. Similar foods can be found in other chapters in this book.

Boiled Groundnuts in the Shell

Wash the freshly harvested nuts thoroughly. Put in a large heavy cooking pot, immerse in water and cover tightly. Boil for one hour. Remove one nut, open it and test whether it is soft. Add salt to taste (1 dsp. per 1 mt. of liquid). Cook for another 30 minutes and drain. Boiled groundnuts are usually served in the shell.

Boiled and Roasted Groundnuts

Prepare Boiled Groundnuts in the Shell as above. Spread on a fine roasting rack over charcoal or over a smoky fire. Turn the groundnuts occasionally, leaving them over the heat until the shells and inner skins are crisp. The groundnuts can be eaten on their own or with boiled corn or farina. Boiled groundnuts can be dried in the oven, but will not have the same smoked flavour.

Baked Shelled Groundnuts

These groundnuts are 'baked' in fine sand in a pot over the fire. Freshly harvested groundnuts are first dried in the sun, then shelled and soaked in salted water (1 dsp. per 2 mgt of water) for 3-4 hours. Drain and dry in the sun or oven. When dry in appearance, mix with fine sand and bake in a cooking pot over a high heat. Sieve to remove the sand. Eat on their own or with soaked garri or farina.

Roasted Groundnuts

Shell the nuts. Heat an iron or clay pot or a heavy frying pan and put the nuts in the hot container. Roast the groundnuts, tossing them with a wooden spoon until golden brown and evenly cooked. Spread on a tray. Cool and remove the papery skin by rubbing between the hands. Add salt to taste and serve alone or with thin slices of roasted coconut, or boiled or roasted corn. Unskinned roasted groundnuts can be lightly oiled and salted, and eaten directly thus increasing their food value.

Sugar-coated Groundnuts
Introduced

Ingredients	Handy Measure	Metric
Roasted groundnuts with skins	1 mt	130 g
Sugar	$\frac{1}{2}$ mt	80 g
Cinnamon, optional	pinch	
Salt	pinch	
Water	$\frac{1}{4}$ mt	45 ml

Melt the sugar in water. Add the groundnuts, cinnamon and salt. Boil until the liquid has evaporated and then stir continuously over a low fire until dry.

Groundnut Butter (Peanut Butter)
Introduced

Ingredients	Handy Measure	Metric
Roasted groundnuts with or without skins*	1 mt	130 g
Groundnut oil, optional	2 dsp	18 ml
Salt	to taste	

* The skins give a pleasant slightly bitter taste.

Lightly salt the groundnuts and warm in a frying pan. Put them in a blender (with oil if necessary, depending on the power of your blender motor). Push the nuts down the sides occasionally. Blend until smooth. This can be done in a mortar. Serve as a spread on bread or in groundnut stews.

Groundnut and Roasted Maize Balls
Hausa: *Dakua*

Fragile but tasty snack treat.

Ingredients	Handy Measure	Metric
Groundnuts	½ mt	65 g
Fine roasted maize meal	½ mt	75 g
Salt	pinch	
Dry ground red pepper	½ tsp	1 g
Sugar	2 dsp	18 g

Roast the groundnuts and remove the papery skins. Pound in a mortar till smooth, add maize meal, salt, pepper and sugar and mix well. Shape, pressing firmly into thick fingers or balls. A few drops of hot water may be added to help to bind the shapes.

Fried Groundnut Balls
Kulinkuli

Pound the roasted shelled groundnuts in a mortar or on a stone until smooth. Collect into a ball, knead and squeeze to remove oil. A little water can be added at each squeeze until most of the oil is extracted. Shape the remaining pulp into balls or shapes of letters of the alphabet. Heat 3 cm deep groundnut oil in a frying pan until it begins to smoke. Fry a few slices of onion in it to flavour. Fry groundnut balls until golden brown. Serve hot or cold.

Spicy Dry Maize Balls
Yoruba: *Adun*

Ingredients	Handy Measure	Metric
Dry maize (not roasted)	1 mt	150 g
Dry ground red pepper	1 tsp	2 g
Onion	2 dsp	18 g
Palm oil	1 dsp	18 ml

Grind the maize (usually unroasted, but roasted maize may be used) in a mill into fine meal. Fry the onion and pepper in palm oil until the onion is well cooked (about 5 minutes). Add the powdered corn. Stir well with the hands and form into balls.

This is sometimes sold along the roadside, wrapped in leaves like eko. In some areas it is served when naming a child: so that the life of the child will be 'as sweet as adun'. It is also a gift at engagement ceremonies.

Boiled Maize and Groundnuts

Ingredients	Handy Measure	Metric
Dried maize	2 mt	300 g
Groundnuts, raw, shelled	1 mt	150 g
Water	8 mt	1.5 l
Salt	to taste	

Soak the maize in water overnight. Wash the maize and groundnuts, put into a cooking pot and add water and salt. Boil until cooked (about 2 hours). Drain and serve hot. This can be cooked in a pressure cooker but care should be taken not to overcook. The seeds should be tender, but separate and firm. Serve hot.

Boiled Maize, Cowpeas and Groundnuts
Yoruba: *Owowo*

Ingredients	Handy Measure	Metric
Cowpeas*	1 mt	125 g
Dry corn	1 mt	125 g
Groundnuts, raw, shelled	1 mt	120 g
Coconut	1 small	500 g
Salt	to taste	
Water		

*Brown type preferred.

If dried corn is used, soak overnight. Cook the corn for 1 hour, then add the cowpeas and cook for 40 minutes. Finally add the groundnuts, salt to taste, and cook for another 30 minutes. Keep covered with water at all times. Drain. All the seeds should be cooked, but separate. Serve with sliced fresh coconut as garnish.
Variation Just cowpeas and maize may be used, if preferred, (Yoruba: *Ayibili*).

Roasted Dry Maize

Heat sand or use hot ashes from charcoal. Put the dry corn into the sand or ash, and stir well. When brown, remove the corn and sprinkle with salt. Serve as a snack.

Roasted Maize and Banana Fritters
Mosa

Ingredients	Handy Measure	Metric
Over-ripe bananas*		
(or plantain)	3 medium	450 g
Ground maize	1 mgt	225 g
Salt	pinch	
Palm oil or vegetable oil	for frying	

* Red type of bananas preferred

Peel the bananas and add the corn and salt, beating thoroughly. Heat the oil and fry small amounts of the batter in the oil, turning when brown. As the mosa fries, it will puff slightly, press with the back of the spoon against the bottom of the pan to remove air. Cool slightly and serve as a snack. Mosa will be crisp and crunchy on the outside and soft in the middle.

Modified Mosa

Ingredients	Handy Measure	Metric
Over-ripe bananas	2	300 g
White wheat flour	½ mt	60 g
Salt	pinch	

Prepare as above.

Ground Dry Maize Confection
Yoruba: *Tanfiri*

Grind roasted corn and mix with granulated sugar to taste. Try 1 dsp. sugar to 1 tpt. ground grains. This is sold in small shot-glass tumblers to school children. Laitan recalls buying it from the 'Anganyi woman at Campbell Street sitting under the almond tree'. Tanfiri can also be made with ground roasted groundnuts and ground roasted rice mixed in equal parts and sweetened to taste with sugar.

Popped Egusi Seeds

Rub a heavy covered pot or skillet lightly with vegetable oil. Heat until a drop of water evaporates immediately it is dropped on it. Pour in a single layer of shelled egusi seeds. Cover and keep the pot shaking gently until all the seeds pop. The colour should be pale brown. Remove immediately and salt lightly.

Fried Egusi Balls
Akara Equsi

Ingredients	Handy Measure	Metric
Egusi, clean, shelled	1 mt	95 g
Onion, ground	1 dsp	9 g
Salt	$\frac{1}{2}$ tsp	
Groundnut oil for frying		

Roast the melon seeds as in previous recipe. Grind the seeds. Knead with the hands until the oil comes out. Mix the onion and salt into the egusi and shape into small round balls (2 cm). Heat the egusi or vegetable oil (deep enough to cover the balls) and fry until golden brown. When cooked, cool the oil and leave the balls in it to absorb more oil. Fried egusi balls are eaten with ogi or eko for breakfast or with soaked garri for a snack.

Fried Over-ripe Plantain
Dodo-Ikire

Ingredients
Over-ripe plantain (black skins)
Salt
Seeds from red peppers (ata rodo, preferred)
Oil for deep frying (preferably palm oil)

Cut the very soft plantain into tiny chunks ($\frac{1}{4}$ mm or less). Lightly salt and blend in the pepper seeds, about 1 dsp. per plantain. Form into small balls, (3 cm in diameter). Flatten slightly and put into hot but not smoking oil. Turn the heat down and cook until the plantain is brown throughout. Remove and drain. Eat while fresh. If the plantain must be reheated, place in a 350°F, 180°C oven for a few minutes or re-fry taking care not to burn it. The patties may tend to break up in the oil. When all the 'bits' of patties are removed and partially cooled, they can be pressed back into patty shapes. In Ikire, where this type of dodo is sold along the roadside, the patties are fried in moulds and unmoulded when cooked, cooled and drained.

Ghanaian Dodo
Kelewele

Ingredients	Handy Measure	Metric
Over-ripe plantain (black skins)	2 fingers	900 g
Tomato paste	1 dsp	18 g
Onion, chopped	2 dsp	18 g
Black pepper	pinch	
Ground dry crayfish	2 dsp	5 g
Dry ground red pepper	to taste	

Cut the plantain into small chunks $\frac{1}{2}$ cm x $\frac{1}{2}$ cm. Blend the remaining ingredients and mix well with the plantain. Heat the oil until it just starts to smoke and add the plantain all at once. Turn the heat down to medium. Cook, turning, until very brown on all sides. Drain well and serve warm.

Over-ripe Plantain Pancake I

Ingredients	Handy Measure	Metric
Over-ripe plantain (black)	3 medium	900 g
Eggs, well beaten	2	
Onion, chopped	$\frac{1}{2}$ medium	75 g
Salt	1 tsp	3 g
Dry ground red pepper	to taste	
Wheat flour	1 mt	125 g

Blend the plantain until smooth. Add the remaining ingredients. Fry by heaped dessertspoonfuls in hot fat until well browned on both sides. Press out the excess oil by using the back of a spoon to push the pancake against the side of the pan. Remove and place on clean absorbent paper. Serve as a snack.

Over-ripe Plantain Pancake II

Ingredients	Handy Measure	Metric
Over-ripe plantain (black)	1	450 g
Flour	3 dsp	9 g
Fresh pepper, chopped	to taste	
Onion, finely chopped	2 dsp	18 g
Garlic	1 clove, crushed	
Ginger	few drops of juice	
Salt	$\frac{1}{4}$ tsp	.75 g
Ground dry crayfish, optional	2 dsp	5 g
Whole small dry crayfish, optional	1 tpt	10 g

Mash or pound the plantain and mix in the flour and remaining ingredients. Drop by dessertspoonfuls in very hot palm or vegetable oil. Press with the back of a spoon to flatten. Fry until brown and then turn and brown the other side. It should take about 15 minutes to cook the plantain well and dry it out somewhat. Press against the side of the pan with the back of the draining spoon. Drain well and serve. It should be crisp on the outside and soft and chewy inside. Not for weight-watchers.

Crisp Fried Green Plantain
Ikpekere

Slice unripe (green) peeled plantain thinly, either across or lengthwise. The thinner the slices, the crisper the product, although traditionally, they were sliced quite thickly (about $\frac{1}{2}$ cm). Salt lightly and fry in palm oil or vegetable oil until lightly browned. Drain the plantain well on absorbent paper and serve as a snack or side dish. Traditionally, the plantain was returned to the oil after cooling slightly, so that it would absorb more oil. For a special effect, Miriam likes to make lengthwise strips with a cheese slicer, and then roll up the strips over her index finger. The rolled slices will retain their shape if they are salted before shaping.

Cowpea Strips

Ingredients	Handy Measure	Metric
Cowpea paste	2 mt	310 g
Wheat flour	½ mt	65 g
Onion	1 small	70 g
Salt	½ tsp	1.5 g
Oil for frying		
Dry ground red pepper	to taste	

Hull the cowpeas and grind to a smooth paste with a minimum of water. Add ground onion, salt, pepper and flour mixing well. The batter should be very thick so that it will hold its shape. Heat the oil and press the mixture through a cake decorator, in strips, into the hot oil. Fry until golden brown and crisp. Serve as finger food at parties. If the paste is too watery, you can squeeze some of the water out through a clean finely woven cloth.

Skillet-roasted Cowpeas

Ingredients	Handy Measure	Metric
Cowpeas	2 mt	250 g
Salt	½ tpt	1 g

Wash the cowpeas and soak for 30 minutes in salted water. Drain and place in a skillet just covered with water, adding ½ tsp. of salt. Cook until the water evaporates, stirring constantly. Continue stirring over the heat until the cowpeas are dry and skins rub off.

Eggs in Cowpea Blankets
Scotch Eggs (introduced)

Ingredients	Handy Measure	Metric
Cowpeas	1½ mt	190 g
Hard boiled eggs	3	
Onion	1 medium	150 g
Nutmeg or curry powder	½ tsp	1 g
Wheat flour	2 dsp	9 g
Salt	½ tsp	1 g

Prepare cowpea paste with the cowpeas, using a minimum of water (see Chapter 3). Add ground onion, seasonings and flour. Coat each boiled egg with the mixture and deep fry in hot oil (375°F, 190°C) until brown. Cut into halves or quarters and serve with a light meal or as a finger food at parties.
Variation: Instead of the cowpea paste mixture, use a yam ball mixture (see Chapter 3) to coat the eggs. Fry in the same way.

Boiled Fluted Pumpkin Seeds

Remove the seeds from a ripe fluted pumpkin. Scrape the outer dark layers with a knife, removing the loose dark fibre and juice. Wash. Immerse in boiling water and cook for 15 minutes. Drain, rinse and break the seeds open. Boil the cream-coloured seeds in clean water for another 15 minutes. Serve with slices of fresh coconut as a snack.

Mixed Roasted Granola
Okenne: *Gorigo*

Prepare a mixture of dry skillet-roasted cowpeas, groundnuts, sesame seeds, etc. (Prepare as Skillet-roasted Cowpeas, opposite). Salt slightly. Serve as a nutritious snack food for children or at cocktail parties.

Mixed Sweet Granola
Introduced

Prepare a mixture of seeds and grains such as those suggested below, in proportions as desired. Salt lightly. For each mt of the mixture, add 2 dsp. or more of honey or any other syrup, and mix well. Bake at 350°F, 180°F for 1 hour, turning to prevent burning. The final product should be brown but not burned. Store in an airtight container. Serve as a snack on its own or with porridge or cold cereals.
Suggested seeds and grains: Grated coconut, roasted groundnuts, skinned or unskinned roasted sesame seeds, popped egusi seeds, popped corn, Quaker oats, roasted cashew nuts, popped rice, raisins, dates.

 ## Fried Snails

See Chapter 6

 ## Fried Beef, Goat-meat or Liver

Cut beef, goat-meat or liver in small bite-sized cubes and fry as for fried meat (See Chapter 4).

 ## Fried Chicken

See Chapter 4

 ## Dry Crayfish

Soak clean small or large dry crayfish from which the heads and tails have been removed in salted water for 15 minutes. Drain. Dry in an oven or over the hearth. Serve as finger food at parties.

 ## Fried Insects and Larvae

A variety of insects and larvae are seasonally popular in some areas. They are fried in their own oil and salted for snacks either alone or with a boiled carbohydrate food. Residents in your locality should be consulted about such local delicacies.

 ## Suya

For each 450 g ($2\frac{1}{2}$ mgt) meat, prepare a mixture of $\frac{1}{2}$ mgt finely chopped groundnuts, $\frac{1}{2}$ tsp. or more dry ground red pepper and $\frac{1}{2}$ tsp. salt. Cut best quality meat into thin ($\frac{1}{2}$ cm or less) slices or small cubes (1-$1\frac{1}{2}$ cm). Coat with the groundnut mixture, pressing it well into the meat. Place the meat on skewers of wood or metal. Cook over charcoal or under a grill until well browned on both sides. Liver may also be prepared this way.
Broomsticks from local brooms can be cleaned and cut in appro-

priate lengths for use in preparing suya or for cocktail 'picks'.
It is possible to buy 'suya skewers' and pre-mixed ground spices (red pepper, ginger, African black pepper and enge) called *Yaji* in the sections of the market selling Hausa foods.

Sandwich Spreads

Sandwiches are a popular food for light meals, for packed lunches and for parties. Sandwiches which contain salad dressing should not be prepared more than a few hours in advance and, even then, should be stored in the refrigerator until used, as many happy occasions have turned into tragedies as a result of food poisoning from salads and sandwich spreads.

There are many popular fillings, including boiled egg, tomato, sardine and corned beef. A few less common fillings which can be easily made are given below. If the sandwich is to contain salad dressing, try boiled dressing (see Chapter 7), rather than a homemade or commercial mayonnaise made with uncooked egg.

Curried Egg Spread

Ingredients	Handy Measure	Metric
Onion	1 medium	150 g
Curry powder	3 dsp	27 g
Vegetable oil	1 dsp	8 ml
Eggs	4 large	
Hard-boiled eggs	2 large	
Breadcrumbs	1 tpt, loosely packed	30 g
Chopped parsley	2 dsp	18 g
Margarine	5 dsp	45 g
Salt, black pepper	to taste	

Fry the onion and curry powder in oil for 3-4 minutes. Stir in the lightly beaten eggs. Cook until scrambled. Chop the hardboiled eggs and parsley finely. Beat all the ingredients together and season to taste. Chill. Spread on bread or serve with toast.

Fish Pâté

Ingredients	Handy Measure	Metric
Flour	½ tpt	25 g
Garlic	1 clove	
Onion	½ tpt, chopped	25 g
Margarine	½ tpt	35 g
African black pepper, ground	1 tsp	2 g
Milk	½ mgt	145 ml
Lemon rind	1 tsp	2 g
Lemon juice	3 dsp	25 ml
Cooked boned fish*	2 mgt	450 g
Salt	1 tsp	3 g

* Try oven-roasted mackerel or any boiled fish. The dark parts of the flesh and skin may or may not be removed according to taste.

Fry the garlic, crushed with the back of a fork in the skillet, and onion in the margarine until the onions are translucent (about 5 minutes). Remove and discard the garlic. Add the flour and blend until well mixed. Add the milk slowly, mixing well. Add black pepper, lemon rind, lemon juice and then the flaked fish. The completed mixture can be mixed well with the back of a spoon or, if a smoother mixture is desired, puréed in an electric mixer. Chill and eat with toast or as a spread on bread.

Cowpea Spread

Ingredients	Handy Measure	Metric
Cowpeas	1 mt	125 g
Onion (finely chopped)	1 dsp	9 g
Lime juice	1 dsp	9 ml
Margarine	2 dsp	9 g
Nutmeg	¼ tsp	.5 g
Salt	1 tsp	3 g

Hull the cowpeas (see Chapter 3). Boil in water until very soft. Drain off any excess water and sieve or blend to a purée. Add all the other ingredients and blend well. Chill. Eat with toast or use as a sandwich spread with sliced tomato, cucumber or chopped green pepper.

Eka's Tuna Salad Substitute

Ingredients	Handy Measure	Metric
Boiled mackerel	1 large	½ kg
Lime juice	from 1 lime	
Commercial mayonnaise or other salad dressings*	1 tpt or more	70 g
Salt and black pepper	to taste	
Finely chopped onion	2 dsp	18 g

* Try boiled salad dressing, Chapter 7.

Cut the mackerel into large pieces and rub each with lime juice and salt. Drain and cool. Remove the skin and dark meat. Mash the light meat well and then blend with the mayonnaise, onion, salt and black pepper to taste. Chill.

Beverages

In a hot climate like ours cool refreshing drinks are always in demand. Unfortunately, the popular commercial carbonated beverages are expensive and of little nutritional value, being composed mainly of sugar, water and flavouring. Commercially prepared fruit squashes are popular and can also be prepared at home.

Hot coffee, tea, chocolate and malt drinks are widely consumed. They are served with bread or other foods for light meals. Tea prepared from lemon grass makes a nice change.

Numerous 'hot (alcoholic) drinks' are prepared in Nigeria from local plants and plant products. Palm wine, the sap of the raffia palm, is very low in alcohol when fresh and contains some vitamins. But the distillates of palm wine (ogogoro, kaikai, local gin, etc) are potent and can, in fact, be toxic. Pito is prepared in many parts of Nigeria; it is a dark brown liquid prepared from fermented maize, sorghum or both. In other areas, distillates of fermented maize, guinea corn and millet are prepared.

The fermented starches prepared from various cereal grains (maize, guinea corn, etc.) which are used thickened with milk and sugar for light food, are also watered down for use as beverages. Local spices and flavourings give variety to such light gruels.

Ginger Beer

Ingredients	Handy Measure	Metric
Fresh succulent ginger roots	1 mgt	350 g
Cloves	3	
Sugar	1½ mt	240 g
Lime or lemon juice	3 dsp	18 ml
Water	3 mgt	870 ml

Scrape and wash the ginger. Put into a mortar and pound. Remove and put in a saucepan with the water. Mash with fingers or a wooden spoon to press out the juice. Put into a finely woven clean white cloth ('tammy') or commercial sieve, and squeeze out the liquid. Dissolve the sugar in the strained liquid and add lemon or lime juice, and cloves. Rest for a few hours. Serve cold.
Alternative method: Boil the crushed ginger, water, clove and sugar for five minutes. Cool and strain.

Fresh Fruit Squashes

Prepare a syrup of 1 mt sugar and 1 mt water by heating until the sugar is dissolved. Then add any of the following fresh fruit preparations. If the squash is to be used immediately it does not need to be cooked. If it is to be stored, bring to the boil and cook for 2 minutes. Cool and bottle. Dilute with water and ice to taste.
Guava Drink   Slice 10 large guavas and add two mt water. Boil for 20 minutes on a low heat. Sieve and add to the syrup.
Pineapple Squash   Blend the chopped flesh from a medium sized fresh pineapple; strain, pressing all the juice out of the pulp. Add the juice of 2 limes or lemons, and 6 cloves or some crushed ginger if desired. Remove the spices before serving.
Pawpaw drink   Chop the flesh from a medium pawpaw and blend to a purée. Sieve and add juice of 12 limes.
Lemonade or Limeade   Add the juice and pulp of 4 well-washed lemons or limes. Serve with a wedge of lemon or lime perched on the edge of the tumbler.
Orange or Grapefruit Squash   Squeeze the juice from 12 well-washed oranges or 6 grapefruits.
Note: Juice is easily extracted from citrus fruits if pressed firmly with the palm of the hand and rolled on a clean surface.

11
Desserts and breads

Traditionally main meals in Nigeria do not include a sweet course, although today fruit may be served at the end of a meal. There are, however, some sweetened snacks and light foods which are eaten at other times. Some of these are included here, with a selection of introduced sweets and baked foods which are becoming more popular, especially for parties. Children should be discouraged from eating between meals, but if snacks are necessary, mothers should be encouraged to offer fruits and the savoury types of snacks given in the last chapter, rather than these which are sweetened with refined sugars.

To give baked goods a nutritional boost, try substituting locally prepared whole grain flours for a quarter of the wheat flour. Millet flour, cowpea flour and plantain flour are particularly nice in breads.

Doughnut Balls
Puff-puff

Ingredients	Handy Measure	Metric
Wheat flour	3 mt	375 g
Fresh palm wine	2 mt	350 ml
Sugar	20 cubes or $\frac{1}{2}$ mt granulated	80 g
Egg optional	1	

Flavouring: 1 tsp. vanilla flavouring, $\frac{1}{2}$ tsp. allspice, $\frac{1}{2}$ tsp. nutmeg or 1 tsp. grated orange rind.

Sift the flour and ground spice, if used. Dissolve the sugar in the palm wine and mix into the flour to make a thick dropping consistency. Add the egg, if used. Beat for 10 minutes to incorporate air. Add the vanilla or orange rind, if used. Place the bowl in a warm place and leave to double in size (about 2 hours). Heat the oil until it begins to smoke. Drop the dough from an oiled dessertspoon into the hot fat. Fry until golden brown; drain well. Serve hot or cold.

Traditional Coconut Biscuit
Gurudi

Crisp wafer-like biscuits, with roasted coconut flavour.

Ingredients	Handy Measure	Metric
Coconut, grated	2 medium	1.6 kg
Sugar	¼ mt	50 g
Edible cassava starch	1 mt	160 g

Mix the starch, finely grated coconut and sugar. If the starch is very dry, a little water may be added to facilitate spreading on the baking tin. Add cinnamon or nutmeg if desired. Spread the mixture thinly on an oiled baking sheet (30 cm x 40 cm). Mark into squares before baking in a medium hot oven (325°F, 170°C). When browned and very dry, cool and put into airtight tins. For a product lighter in colour, use a lower temperature and bake longer until well dried.

Chin-Chin

These are small, crunchy chunks of fried sweetened dough.

Ingredients	Handy Measure	Metric
Wheat flour	1 mt	125 g
Granulated sugar	¼ mt	30 g
Eggs	2 small	
Milk or water to bind	as needed	
Flavouring (nutmeg or grated lemon rind)	1 tsp	

Sift the flour and make a well in the centre. Beat the eggs, sugar and flavourings and mix into the flour. Add sufficient milk or water to bind into a stiff dough and knead until smooth. Roll out ¼ - ½ cm thick and cut into strips, cubes or small triangles. Heat the oil until it smokes and fry the pastry until it browns. Drain and cool. Store in an airtight container.

Coconut-Cassava Biscuits
Beju

Ingredients	Handy Measure	Metric
Fresh cassava	2 mgt	180 g
Sugar	4 dsp	35 g
Grated coconut	1 mt	150 g

Grate the peeled raw cassava and squeeze out the excess starchy water with the hands or through a fine muslin cloth. Sieve the pulp and then mix well with the sugar, a pinch of salt and the grated coconut. Bake in rings on a greased baking sheet at 275°F, 140°C. When set, remove, turn, and continue baking until dry and browned.

Coconut Biscuits (Cookies)

Ingredients	Handy Measure	Metric
Butter or margarine	½ mt	120 g
Granulated sugar	½ mt	80 g
Grated coconut, packed	½ mt	80 g
Lemon juice	1 tsp	3 ml
Lemon or orange rind, grated	1 tsp	3 g
Sifted wheat flour	1½ mt	190 g
Baking powder	¼ tsp	2 g
Egg	1	

Cream the butter or margarine and sugar. Stir in the coconut, lemon juice, rind and beaten egg. Add the sifted dry ingredients and mix thoroughly. Roll out thinly and cut into shapes or form into small balls, flattened with the fingers or the bottom of a lightly oiled tumbler. Bake on a flat baking sheet at 325°F, 170°C, for 7-10 minutes or until lightly browned. Cool and store in an airtight tin. These biscuits should be brown and crisp when cool.

Garri Biscuits (Cookies)

Ingredients	Handy Measure	Metric
Wheat flour	2 mt	250 g
Fine sieved garri	1 mt	100 g
Baking powder	1 tsp	3 g
Margarine	1 mt	190 g
Grated lemon or orange rind	1 tsp	2 g
Egg	1	
Granulated sugar	1 mt	80 g

Sift the dry ingredients. Rub the margarine into the mixture and bind with the beaten egg and lemon juice. Roll out very thinly, pricking with a fork, and cut into shapes or roll into small balls and flatten with the oiled bottom of a tumbler. Bake at 325°F, 170°C, for 15 minutes or until pale brown. Cool and store in an airtight tin. These biscuits should be crisp when cool.

Coconut Biscuits (Cookies)
Chukchuk

Ingredients	Handy Measure	Metric
Grated coconut (pressed)	1 mt	160 g
Egg yolks	2	
Sugar	4 dsp	35 g

The coconut may be freshly grated or more commonly the residue left from making coconut milk may be used. Mix the coconut, sugar, and egg yolks. Form into balls 2 cm in diameter (about 1 dsp. each). Roll each ball in flour and place on an oiled baking sheet. Bake at 325°F, 170°C, until golden brown. Cool and store in an airtight tin.

Coconut Groundnut Biscuits

Ingredients	Handy Measure	Metric
Groundnut butter	1 mt	250 g
Grated coconut, packed	1 mt	160 g
Wheat flour	2 mt	250 g
Egg	1	
Granulated sugar	¼ mt	40 g
Margarine	½ tpt or 4 dsp	35 g
Salt	½ tsp	1.5 g
Bicarbonate of soda	pinch	

Mix all the ingredients together adding the beaten egg to make a stiff paste. Roll out very thinly and cut into shapes. Prick with a fork and bake at 325°F, 170°C, until light brown. Remove from the pan and cool. The biscuits should be crisp. Store in an airtight tin.

Wholemeal Oat Biscuits (Cookies)

Ingredients	Handy Measure	Metric
Wholemeal flour	1 mt	125 g
Brown sugar	¾ mt	120 g
Margarine	¾ mt	120 g
Rolled oats	1 mt	100 g
Salt	pinch	

Melt the margarine and mix all the ingredients well with the hands. Press thinly into an oiled tin. Bake at 300°F, 150°C, until browned (about 30 minutes). Cut while warm. When cool remove and store in an airtight tin. These biscuits are dry, crisp and very sweet — more like a confection.

Grated Carrot Cake

Ingredients	Handy Measure	Metric
Margarine	½ mt	100 g
Granulated sugar	1 mt	156 g
Eggs	2	
Salt	½ tsp	1.5 g
Grated lemon peel	½ tsp	1 g
Cinnamon	½ tsp	1 g
Wheat flour	2 mt	250 g
Grated carrots	2 mt	250 g
Baking powder	3 tsp	9 g

Beat the margarine and sugar until creamy and light coloured. Add the beaten eggs and lemon peel. Mix in the sifted flour, cinnamon and baking powder. Fold in the grated carrot. Bake at 350°F, 180°C, in small loaf pans three-quarters full for 40 minutes or until lightly browned and the surface springs back when pressed lightly with a finger.

Fresh Cassava and Coconut Cake

A 'gummy' textured cake, with a crisp brown top. Adapted from a Philippine recipe. Popular with children.

Ingredients	Handy Measure	Metric
Fresh grated raw cassava	1 mgt	150 g
Whole coconut	1 medium	700 g
Sugar	1 mt	150 g

Grate the coconut coarsely and pour over 2 mt of boiling water. Steep for several minutes. Mix the grated cassava with the coconut and water, add sugar and stir well. Pour into a greased baking dish to a depth of 3 cm. Bake at 250°F, 130°C, for 4 hours until firm and well browned on top.

Pamela's Banana Cake

Ingredients	Handy Measure	Metric
Granulated sugar	$\frac{1}{4}$ mt	40 g
Margarine	1 mt	200 g
Wheat flour	2 mt	250 g
Baking powder	2 tsp	6 g
Eggs	2	
Banana, mashed	3 small or $1\frac{1}{2}$ mt	150 g

Cream the sugar and margarine until light in colour. Stir in the sifted flour and baking powder. Add the beaten egg and mashed banana. Bake in a small loaf tin three-quarters full at 350°F, 180°C, for 30 minutes or until it is lightly brown and springs back when pressed with a finger.

Sponge Cake Made with Oil

Ingredients	Handy Measure	Metric
Eggs	2 large	
Granulated sugar	2 mt + 2 dsp	340 g
White wheat flour	2 mt	250 g
Baking powder	4 dsp	9 g
Salt	1 tsp	3 g
Vegetable oil	1 mt	70 ml
Milk	1 mt + 3 dsp	225 ml
Flavouring (vanilla, lemon or orange rind)	1 tsp	

Heat the oven to 350°F, 180°C. Oil and lightly flour two sponge tins or a large oblong tin. Separate the eggs and whip the whites until frothy. Gradually beat one-third of the sugar into the whites and whip until smooth. Set this meringue aside. Sift the flour. Blend the flour, sugar, baking powder and salt. Add the oil, half the milk and flavouring. Beat for 1 minute with a mixer or 150 strokes by hand. Add the remaining milk and egg yolks. Beat for 1 more minute. Fold in the meringue. Pour into baking tins. Bake the layers for 30-35 minutes or the oblong tin for 40-45 minutes, until well browned. Cool. Serve with custard or lemon curd filling (see below).

Lemon Curd Filling

Ingredients	Handy Measure	Metric
Sugar	1 mt + 1 dsp	165 g
Cornflour	4 dsp	30 g
Salt	$\frac{1}{3}$ dsp	1 g
Water	$2\frac{1}{2}$ tpt	170 ml
Margarine	2 dsp	15 g
Lemon, juice	2 lemons	
Grated lemon rind	3 dsp	6 g
Eggs	3 yolks or 1 egg and 1 yolk	

Mix the sugar, cornstarch and salt in a saucepan. Gradually stir in the water and bring to the boil, stirring constantly. Boil for 1 minute. Stir half the mixture into the well-beaten eggs. Blend into the remaining cornstarch mixture. Remove from the heat and add butter, lemon rind and juice. Mix well and cool. Serve as a cake filling or spread on bread.

Coconut Candy

Ingredients	Handy Measure	Metric
Fresh root ginger, chopped finely	1-3 dsp	
Granulated sugar	4 mt	625 g
Grated coconut, pressed	2 mt	215 g
Water	$\frac{1}{2}$ mt	90 ml

Heat the sugar and water in a heavy saucepan. Add coconut and ginger. Cook until a drop forms a soft ball in a tumbler of cold water. Drop quickly in mounds on to a wet plate or lightly oiled flat baking sheet. Allow to harden. Wrap individually or store in an airtight container. The cooked coconut candy can also be poured on to a baking sheet, spread slightly and allowed to cool. Break into pieces for storage.

Custards

Introduced Puddings

Thickened starch-based foods of thick pouring consistency are prepared traditionally in Nigeria with fermented starch from maize (ogi) and other grains as well. These may or may not be served with sugar and/or milk. Today custard powder (flavoured cornstarch) is very popular with babies and children and as a topping for desserts. When prepared with milk, these soft foods have some nutritional value in addition to supplying energy. The food value of any of them can be increased by the addition of a beaten egg on removing from the heat. A few homemade custard recipes are given below for variety.

Coconut and Fermented Cornstarch Porridge

Kanjika

Ingredients	Handy Measure	Metric
Ogi	2 tpt	180 g
Coconut milk (from flesh of 1 coconut)	4 tpt	280 ml
Sugar	½ mt	80 g
Cinnamon, nutmeg or grated coconut	to taste	

Prepare as for eko (see Chapter 3) but use coconut milk instead of water. Add sugar and flavourings to the coconut milk before cooking. Mould in leaves or decorative jelly moulds and cool.

Farina Porridge
Mengun

Ingredients	Handy Measure	Metric
Fine farina	1½ mt	100 g
Coconuts	3 small	1.5 kg
Sugar	to taste	

Flavouring: 1 tsp. grated nutmeg, 1 tsp. allspice or 4-6 cloves.

Prepare the coconut milk from the coconuts using 6 mt of water (see Chapter 2). Soak the farina overnight in the cool coconut milk. Cook the mixture until the tapioca becomes soft and transparent. Flavour with nutmeg, clove and/or allspice. Sweeten with sugar to taste. Cook for another 2 minutes. Serve hot in small bowls, with or without milk, accompanied by bread and butter for breakfast.

Rice Porridge (Pudding)
Yoruba: *Arosidosi*

Ingredients	Handy Measure	Metric
Rice	1 mt	130 g
Coconut	2 medium	1.6 kg
Sugar	to taste (10-15 cubes)	

Flavouring: vanilla, coconut and/or nutmeg, or sweetened chocolate drinking powder.

Prepare the coconut milk (see Chapter 2) using 4 mt of water. Boil the rice in the coconut milk in a covered pan over low heat until very soft. Add sugar. Sprinkle lightly with flavourings as desired. Cool. Use as a dessert.

Blancmange (Cornstarch Custard)

Ingredients	Handy Measure	Metric
Sugar	⅓ mt	60 g
Cornflour	4½ dsp	40 g
Milk	2½ mt	270 ml
Vanilla flavouring	1½ tsp	4.5 ml

Mix the sugar and cornflour with a little milk. Heat the remainder of the milk and pour over the blended cornflour. Return to the saucepan and cook over a medium heat, stirring constantly, until the mixture boils. Cook for 1 minute. Remove from the heat and stir in the vanilla. Cool. Serve chilled.

Rich Custard (Crème à la Vanille)

Ingredients	Handy Measure	Metric
Egg yolks	4	
Milk	2½ mt	280 ml
Sugar	½ mt	75 g
Vanilla	1 tsp	3 ml

Put the sugar and milk in a double boiler or arrange a cooking pan over another pan containing 2 cms of boiling water. By placing it over boiling water the custard will cook in the steam.
Beat the egg yolks with a fork. Heat the milk and sugar in the top of the double boiler to boiling point. Pour on to yolks, stir, and return to the pan. Stir until the liquid will coat the back of the spoon. Pour off and add vanilla when nearly cool.

Baked Custard

Ingredients	Handy Measure	Metric
Eggs	2 whole and 2 yolks	
Milk	2½ mt	280 ml
Sugar	½ mt	75 g
Grated nutmeg	to taste	

Break the eggs into a bowl, add yolks and sugar and beat well with a fork. Scald milk and pour on to egg mixture, stir and pour into a greased dish. Dot with a little butter and sprinkle with nutmeg. Stand the dish in a baking dish of water and bake at 350°F, 180°C for one hour or more until set
To 'bake' in a pressure cooker, use a glass baking dish or 'congo' enamel bowl. Cover tightly with tinfoil and place on a rack in the pressure cooker. Add 1 cm of water, bring to 15 pounds pressure and cook for 5 minutes. Release pressure quickly under cold running water.

Baked Ripe Plantain and Crushed Groundnuts

Ingredients	Handy Measure	Metric
Ripe plantain	2 medium	600 g
Finely chopped roasted groundnuts	1 mt	100 g

Peel the plantain, by slitting once lengthwise. Replace the flesh in the skin and cut each into two across. Place on a greased baking sheet and bake until brown. Open the skins and sprinkle with chopped groundnuts. Serve as a dessert. A little honey or other syrup may be poured over if desired.

Simple Coconut Cream Gelatine

Ingredients	Handy Measure	Metric
Coconut	1 medium	800 g
Sugar	$\frac{1}{4}$ mt	45 g
Gelatine	3 dsp	25 g
Dried milk	$\frac{1}{2}$ mt	60 g

Prepare the coconut milk with $1\frac{1}{2}$ mt of water (see Chapter 2). Cool and add the dried milk and sugar. Soften the gelatine in a few dessertspoons of cold water, then add $\frac{1}{2}$ mt boiling water to dissolve. Stir into the coconut milk mixture. Pour into moulds and refrigerate until set. Unmould to serve.

Crème Caramel

Ingredients	Handy Measure	Metric
Caramel		
Sugar	$\frac{1}{2}$ mt	75 g
Custard		
Eggs	2 whole and 2 yolks	
Milk	$2\frac{1}{2}$ mt	280 ml
Sugar	$\frac{1}{2}$ mt	75 g
Vanilla	1 tsp	3 ml

Put $\frac{1}{2}$ mt of white granulated sugar in a very heavy metal (not iron) pan over a very low heat without stirring until the sugar has melted. When it begins to change colour stir carefully from time to time until a golden brown. Pour into a warmed ovenproof dish. Turn it about to coat the caramel over the bottom and sides. Break the eggs into a bowl, add yolks, sugar and vanilla and beat with a fork. Scald milk and pour on eggs, stir and pour into the caramel coated tin. Stand in a baking dish of water. Cover with greaseproof paper and bake at 350°F, 180°C for one hour or more until set. Remove from heat and leave until cold before turning out.

Coconut Bread

Ingredients	Handy Measure	Metric
Coconut, grated	1 medium	800 g
Wheat flour	4 mt	500 g
Melted margarine	$\frac{1}{2}$ mt	100 g
Milk and/or coconut water	$\frac{1}{4}$ mt	50 ml
Granulated sugar	$\frac{1}{2}$ mt	80 g
Vanilla	1 tsp	3 ml
Baking powder	4 tsp	12 g
Raisins, optional	$\frac{1}{2}$ mt	70 g
Egg	1	
Salt	$\frac{1}{2}$ tsp	1.5 g

Sift the dry ingredients. Add the sugar, beaten egg, milk and margarine. Stir in coconut and raisins. Blend well. Shape into two large loaves or 3 small ones ($\frac{1}{2}$-$\frac{3}{4}$ full). Bake at 325°F, 170°C, for an hour or more until golden brown. Cool. Serve sliced thinly with butter or margarine.

Rice Bread

Ingredients	Handy Measure	Metric
Ground rice	1 mgt	225 g
Fresh banana	1 medium	150 g
Milk	1 mgt	290 ml
Sugar	1 mt	150 g
Nutmeg	pinch	

Use commercially prepared or home-ground rice. Mash the bananas and mix with the ground rice. Add sugar, nutmeg and milk. Bake at 325°F, 170°C, for 1 hour in a cake tin. When cooked the cake should be well browned and firm to the touch. Serve warm as a dessert or with tea.

Cowpea Tea Cake

Ingredients	Handy Measure	Metric
Cowpea flour	$\frac{1}{2}$ mt	60 g
Wheat flour	1 mt	125 g
Eggs	2	
Margarine	$\frac{1}{4}$ mt	50 g
Sugar, granulated	$\frac{1}{4}$ mt	40 g
Nutmeg, ground	$\frac{1}{2}$ tsp	1 g
Salt	$\frac{1}{2}$ tsp	1.5 g
Baking powder	1 tsp	1.5 g
Water	$\frac{1}{3}$ mt	

Cream the margarine, sugar and salt until frothy. Add the eggs and beat well. Add the nutmeg. Sift the dry ingredients and fold into the creamed mixture. Add $\frac{1}{3}$ mt of water. Put the mixture into small cupcake tins or loaf tins, three-quarters full. Bake at 350°F, 180°C, for about 20-40 minutes, or until browned on top and the surface springs back when pressed. Cool. This is like a tea bread and can be served warm with butter.

Rice and Plantain Loaf

Ingredients	Handy Measure	Metric
Peeled over-ripe plantain	4 mt	800 g
Soft-cooked boiled rice	2 mt	400 g
Wheat flour	1 mt	125 g
Granulated sugar	1 mt	120 g
Margarine	1 mt	200 g
Milk	1 mt	190 ml
Grated nutmeg, optional	1 tsp	2 g
Currants, optional	$\frac{1}{2}$ mt	75 g
Eggs	2	
Vanilla	1 tsp	3 ml

Cream the sugar and margarine until light in colour. Add the eggs and beat well. Add the remaining ingredients and blend thoroughly. Put into a greased baking tin three-quarters full and bake at 350°F, 180°C, for 1½ hours or until lightly browned and the surface springs back when pressed lightly with the finger.

Orange Bread

Ingredients	Handy Measure	Metric
Wheat flour	4 mt	500 g
Baking powder	6 tsp	5 g
Granulated sugar	½ mt	80 g
Juice of one orange	3 dsp	18 ml
Grated orange rind	2 tsp	4 g
Melted margarine or oil	½ tpt	35 ml
Milk	1 mt	90 ml
Eggs	2	

Sift the flour with the salt, baking powder and sugar. Beat the eggs well and add the milk. Stir the eggs and milk into the dry ingredients and add the orange peel. Put the mixture into two small loaf pans three-quarters full and bake at 350°F, 180°C, for 1 hour or until well browned.

Pawpaw Muffins
Tea-bread in cupcake tins

Ingredients	Handy Measure	Metric
Diced pawpaw (almost ripe)	1 mt	150 g
Margarine	⅓ mt	70 g
Sugar	⅓ mt	50 g
Egg	1	
Salt	½ tsp	1.5 g
Milk	⅔ mt	125 ml
Wheat flour	1½ mt	188 g
Baking powder	2 tsp	6 g
Cinnamon	¼ tsp	.5 g
Nutmeg, optional	pinch	

Cream the margarine and sugar until light and creamy. Beat in the egg. Add the dry ingredients and milk and stir lightly to mix: do not beat. Finally, gently fold in the chopped pawpaw. Half fill cupcake tins. Mix ¼ tsp. cinnamon, a pinch of ground nutmeg, if desired, and 3 dsp. sugar. Sprinkle over the tops of the muffins before baking. Bake at 375°F, 190°C, for 20 minutes. Best served warm with butter.

White Bread

Ingredients	Handy Measure	Metric
Flour	2 mgt	300 g
Dried yeast	1 tsp	3 g
Salt	1 tsp	3 g
Sugar	½ tsp	1.5 g
Water		175 ml

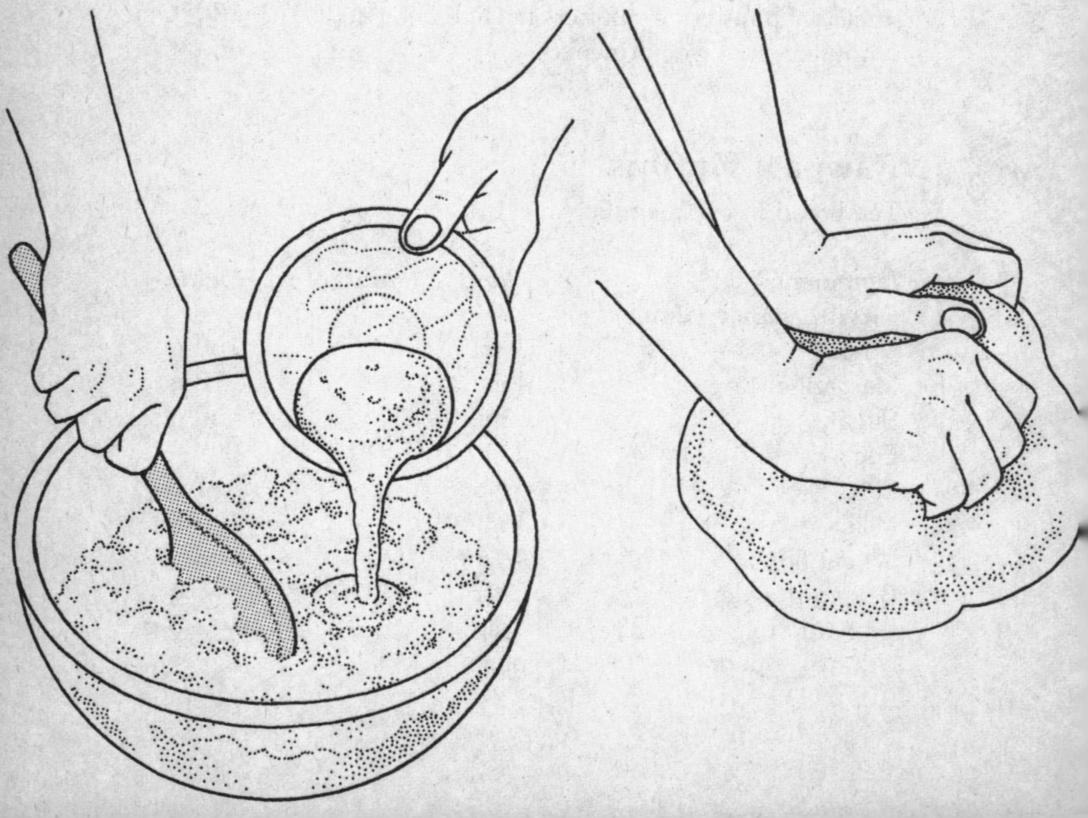

Dissolve ½ tsp. of sugar in a cup of warm water (taken from the 175 ml). Sprinkle the dried yeast on top and leave until frothy (about 10 minutes). Put the flour and salt in a large bowl. Add the activated yeast and the rest of the water. Mix to a soft dough which leaves the bowl clean. Knead thoroughly on a floured table top pushing the dough away from you with the palm of the hand. Continue for about ten minutes until the dough feels firm and elastic and does not stick to the fingers. Put the dough in a greased bowl, cover with a cloth and leave in a warm place until doubled in size (1-2 hours). Knead well again, cover and leave to rise again until almost doubled (about 1 hour). Divide into two and shape each half into a loaf and put in a greased loaf tin. Cover with a cloth and leave to rise (about $\frac{1}{2}$ hour). Put loaves in a hot oven at 425°F, 220°C, and bake for 25-30 minutes or until deep golden brown. The loaf will retract slightly from the sides and should sound hollow when tapped. Remove bread from pans immediately and place on a rack to cool.

Rich Egg Bread

Follow instructions for White Bread but use milk instead of water and add 50 g margarine and three beaten eggs.

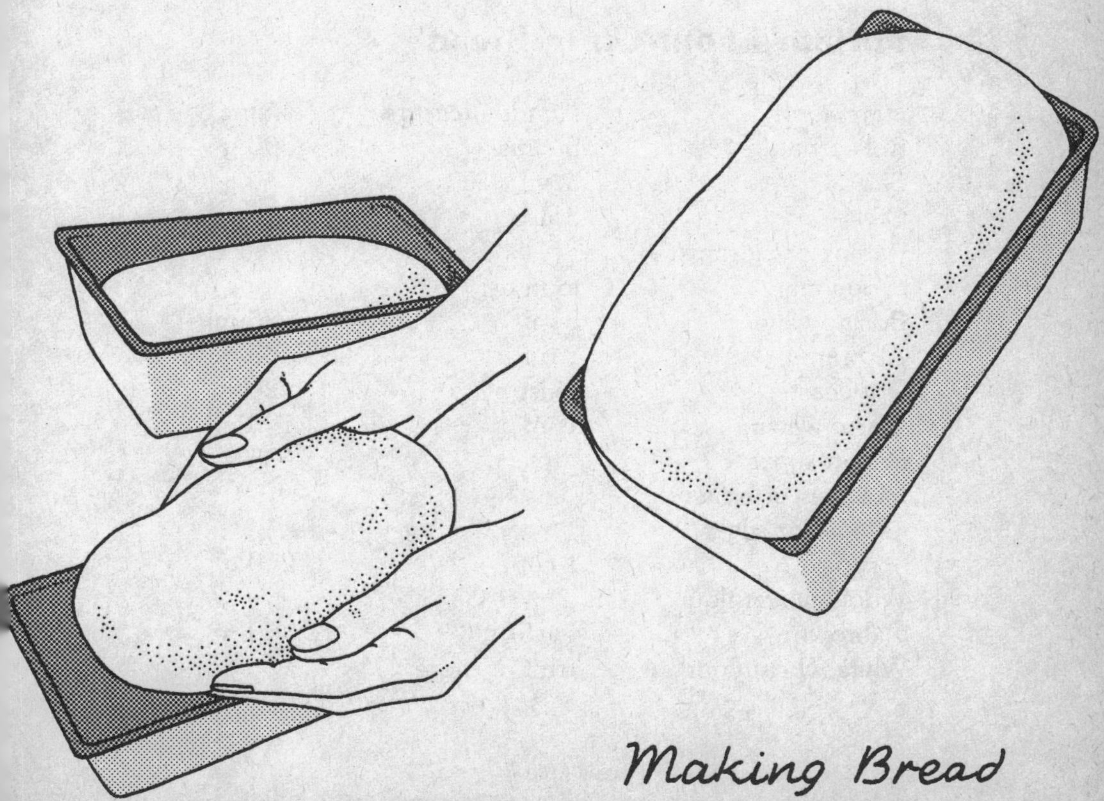

Making Bread

Whole Grain Bread

Ingredients	Handy Measure	Metric
Whole grain flour	2 mgt	300 g
White wheat flour	1 mgt	150 g
Dried yeast	1½ tsp	4.5 g
Salt	1½ tsp	4.5 g
Honey, brown sugar or molasses	1 tsp	
Margarine	2 dsp	25 g
Warm milk and water	1 mgt	290 ml

Soften the yeast in warm milk and water. Add the margarine, salt, honey and half the flours. Beat well for five minutes or for two minutes with an electric mixer. Add the remaining flour and blend well. Cover with a cloth and leave to rise until doubled in size, about 1 hour. Stir down batter which will be sticky and pour into a greased loaf tin. Allow to rise until doubled in size. Bake at 375°F, 190°C, for 45-50 minutes or until brown. Remove from tins, brush with oil and cool on a rack.

Miriam's Four-Grain Bread

Ingredients	Handy Measure	Metric
Rolled oats	3 cups	300 g
Salt	3 tsp	9 g
Oil	3 dsp	25 ml
Raisins or currants, optional	to taste	
Boiling water	3 mt	570 ml
All bran	2 mt	100 g
Dry yeast	3 dsp	20 g
Warm water	1 mt	190 ml
Brown sugar	½ tpt	35 g
Molasses or brown sugar or sugar syrup	1 cup	250 g
Whole wheat flour (brown)	4½-5½ mt	560-680 g
White wheat flour	1 mt or more	125 g +

Combine the first six ingredients; allow to cool until lukewarm. Blend the next four ingredients in a separate bowl and set aside until foamy (spongy). Combine the two lukewarm mixtures. Add molasses and whole wheat flour and mix well. Then add enough white flour to make a soft dough, so that it can be kneaded lightly. Let the dough rise until it doubles in size. Divide into four parts and place in loaf pans. Let rise until light. Bake at 350°F, 180°C, for 1 hour. The bread is done when it is well browned and sounds hollow when tapped with the fist. It will have withdrawn somewhat from the sides of the tin. Cool and slice. This bread can be kept in the refrigerator for a few days.

Yeast Rolls with Millet or Guinea Corn Flour

Ingredients	Handy Measure	Metric
Water	1½ mt	300 ml
Margarine or vegetable oil	⅓ mt	70 g
Brown or white sugar	⅓ mt	50 g
Salt	1 tsp	3 g
Guinea corn or millet flour	3 mt	400 g
Egg	1	
Dry yeast	3 dsp	20 g
Wheat flour	5 mt	600 g
Dry milk powder	¾ mt	100 g

Soften the yeast in ½ mt of warm water. Mix 1 mt of boiling water with the milk powder, margarine, sugar, salt and guinea corn flour. Cool slightly. Mix in the beaten egg and yeast. Finally add sufficient wheat flour to make an easily handled dough. Shape into rolls and place on an oiled flat baking sheet or put into oiled cupcake tins. Allow to rise until doubled in size. Bake at 350°F, 180°C, for 30 minutes or until well browned.

Fruits

Fresh fruits are most appealing when of the best quality and served simply. Thus, a full quarter of a medium-sized pawpaw with or without its skin, seeds removed, could be served with a wedge or half of a small lime. A carefully peeled pineapple could be served in thick slices with or without thick yoghurt as an accompaniment. An orange could be served chilled, with only the oily outer yellow or green surface removed. There are numerous other fruits which are available seasonally.

A common way of serving fruits is in fruit salad. This can be nice but the distinctiveness of the fruits is often lost if the pieces are cut too fine, if the fruit is over-ripe or if it is prepared too far in advance of use. Bananas and avocado pear should be added just before serving. Other fruits which can be used include guava (seeds removed), orange, grapefruit, pineapple, pawpaw, grated coconut, lime juice, pitanga cherries and mango.

Stewed Guavas

Ingredients	Handy Measure	Metric
Seeded guava slices	2 mgt	225 g
Granulated sugar	1 mt	160 g
Water	$\frac{1}{2}$ mt	95 ml
Lemon juice	2 dsp	18 ml

Wash, peel, halve, seed and slice the guavas. Boil the sugar, lemon juice and water to form a syrup. Add the guavas and cook slowly until just tender, but not mushy. Remove carefully and serve with cream.

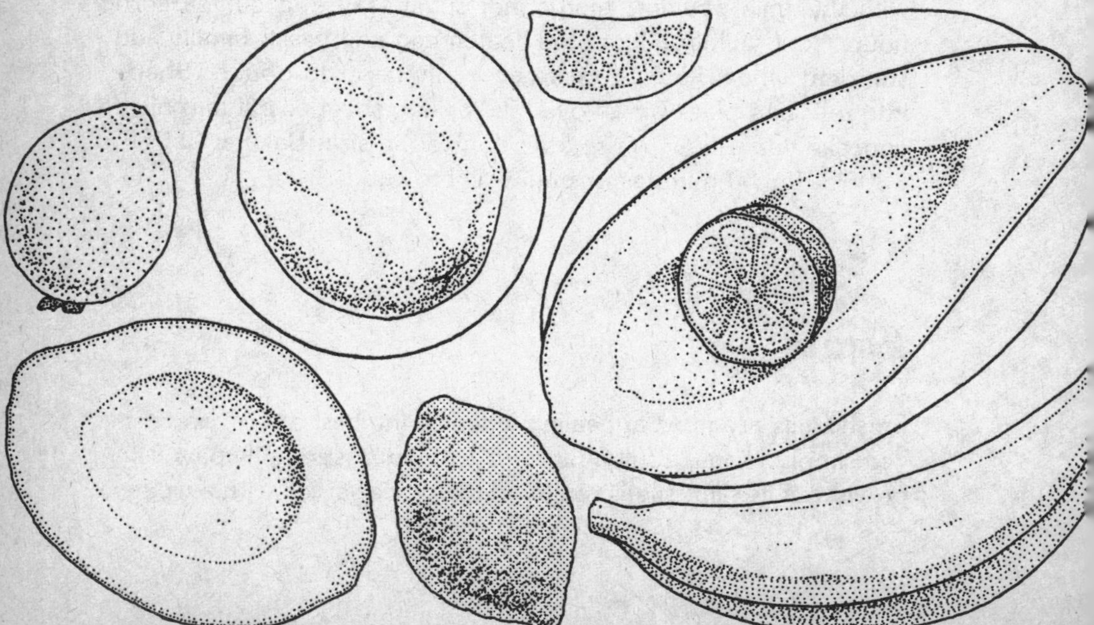

Guava Purée

Press stewed guavas through a sieve. Serve with cream.

Pineapple Ice (Sherbet)

Ingredients	Handy Measure	Metric
Granulated sugar	1 mt	160 g
Water	2 mt	380 ml
Lemon juice	½ mt	90 ml
Crushed pineapple	2 mt	400 g
Salt	pinch	

Blend all the ingredients and freeze to a mush. Whisk with a mixer or wire whisk. Re-freeze.

Jams

Jams for spreading on bread or for filling doughnuts or sponge layers are popular in Nigeria, but they are limited in variety and increasingly expensive. Use heavy aluminium, enamel or stainless steel pans, rather large in size to facilitate quick cooking. To test

Serving Fruit

the jam, remove the pan from the heat; cool a drop on a plate. If the surface wrinkles when pushed with the finger, it is done. If a sugar thermometer is available, cook until 220°F, 122°C. In our climate, it is safer to make small quantities and to store jam in the refrigerator rather than to attempt to seal the jars and to store them for long periods.

Pawpaw Jam

Boil green, partly ripe or ripe peeled pawpaw (according to taste) in water to just cover, until soft. Blend or sieve. Mix equal parts pawpaw pulp and sugar in a pan. Boil quickly until very thick (about 15 minutes). When thick, pour into sterilized jars and cool. Store in a refrigerator. Orange juice can be used instead of water, or a dsp. grated lemon rind or $\frac{1}{2}$ tsp. cinnamon added with the sugar.

Mixed Fruit Jam

Mix 1 mt each: finely chopped banana, mango or pawpaw, and pineapple. Add a dsp. grated lemon or orange peel if desired. Add $\frac{3}{4}$ mt water and boil for 5 minutes. Add $3\frac{1}{2}$ mt sugar and boil until very thick (about 15 minutes). Pour into sterilized jars and cool. Store refrigerated.

Guava Jam

Wash, peel and slice under-ripe guavas. Just cover with water Boil until fruit is soft. Sieve. Measure the thick juice and add 1 mt sugar and 1 tsp. lime juice for each mt juice. Heat juice, add sugar and lime juice. Boil quickly (rolling boil) until mixture sets. Pour into sterilized jars and cool.

Pineapple Jam

Cook 2 mgt grated pineapple and 1 mgt water gently until the fruit is soft. Add $1\frac{1}{2}$ mgt granulated sugar and a dsp. lime juice. Cook until thick and set. Cool and bottle. Store refrigerated.

12

Nutritionally balanced menus

Most of the traditional combinations of foods eaten by Nigerians in the past provided a balanced diet when they were cooked well. However, this was not always the case because in some areas, there was a general lack of appreciation of vegetables, while in others there was a lack of animal protein, and in yet others a lack of animal or plant protein.

Traditionally one main meal was eaten each day, with one or two other light meals as an accompaniment. Most of these foods were eaten at any time of the day. Although there were many exceptions, on the whole boiled foods were often eaten with thinner stews and pepper soups, while thicker stews and those with 'draw' were taken with thickened carbohydrate foods such as amala, eba, fufu, pounded yam, tuwo etc. Rice did not usually accompany foods with 'draw' unless mashed as in tuwo.

Today, particularly in urban areas, most families have a heavy mid-afternoon meal (after work) and light meals before work and in the early evening before bed. It is important that the first meal of the day should give workers, home-makers and children a good start. It should include some good quality protein such as meat or fish, milk, egg and/or cowpeas. The main meal should be well balanced and contain protein, vitamins and minerals as well as the large amounts of carbohydrate usually consumed. Green vegetables, fresh or cooked, and fresh fruits should be included if possible. The evening meal should be light and relatively low in carbohydrate to encourage sleep. Children who tend to eat snacks between meals should be taught to appreciate the many unsweetened snack foods and fruits which are available (see Chapter 10).

Many traditional combinations of foods and modern variations have been mentioned in the recipes which have appeared earlier in this book. The following menus are simply suggestions which may or may not be traditional, but which the authors think will provide a healthy diet.

Breakfast and light meals

Try these various combinations of a mainly carbohydrate food and a protein-containing one. For a more balanced meal, add some fresh fruit.

Carbohydrate	Protein-containing Food
Ogi or eko	Moyin-moyin Soft boiled cowpeas
Roasted ripe plantain	Groundnuts Fried fish
Soaked garri or farina	Roasted groundnuts Dry fish or crayfish Fresh roasted prawns
Bread	Akara Omelettes Groundnuts Simple palm-oil stews
Steamed plantain or maize pudding	Dry fish or crayfish
Boiled yam, cocoyam, wateryam or green plantain Fried yam or cocoyam	Omelette or fried eggs Simple palm oil stew with fish or meat Simple palm oil stew with fish or meat Simple steamed cowpea paste (ekuru) Beef or Dry Fish Pepper Soup

Main Meals

One-dish Meals

These foods are traditionally served alone. Try serving them with a vitamin-rich side dish such as a salad or fresh fruit.
Mashed Cocoyam and Palm Oil
Pork and Green Plantain Pottage
Liver, Yam and Ripe Plantain Pottage
Thick Goat Meat Pottage with Green Plantain
Thick Goat Meat Pepper Soup with Green Plantain and Yam
Chicken Jollof Rice

Grated Cocoyam in Leaves with Dry Fish and Meat
Dry Fish and Dry Crayfish Yam Pottage
Thickened Wateryam Soup with Dry Fish
Dry Fish and Rice Casserole
Dry Fish Plantain Pottage

Two-dish Meals with Thickened Carbohydrate

Most of these meals which comprise a thickened carbohydrate and a protein-containing stew are nutritionally balanced.

Thickened Carbohydrate	*Protein/Vitamin-Rich Dish*
Imoyo eba	Marinated (Imoyo) chicken or fish
Cassava fufu	Steamed greens with dry fish Groundnut stew with fresh groundnuts and dry fish Bitterleaf stew with meat and stockfish
Soft boiled rice (tuwo shinkafa)	Quick okro and locust bean soup Dried okro and groundnut fish soup Beans and okro soup Herbed egusi soup with beef and liver
Cassava starch	Dry crayfish agbono soup Any banga soup Any thickened pepper soup
Pounded yam	Fresh shrimp and okro soup Chicken and okro soup Dry fish and egusi-ball soup
Eba	Okazi soup Dry fish and wateryam ball pottage Frejon with meat Agbono with fresh fish and locust bean

Thickened ground millet	Dry fish, fresh fish, and dry okro soup (kuka soup) Any leafy green vegetable soup with meat or dry fish
Steamed ground rice	Beef, fresh fish or dry fish palm oil stew
Eko	Cowpea and plantain pottage

Two-dish Meals with Boiled Carbohydrate

Most of these meals could be improved nutritionally by the addition of a cooked vegetable, salad or fresh fruit.

Boiled Carbohydrate	*Protein/Vitamin-Rich Soup or Stew*
Boiled cocoyam	Any pepper soup Uncooked fried agbono soup Fried shrimp
Boiled green plantain	Goat meat or dry fish or chicken pepper soup Fresh fish and prawn pepper soup Sautéed periwinkles and fresh shrimps
Simple Jollof Rice	Roast or fried fish, chicken or pork
Coconut rice	Roast or fried fish or chicken Marinated pork cubes
Boiled yam	Groundnut stew Dry crayfish pepper soup Dry fish 'butter' Shrimps steamed in banana leaves (side dish of best palm oil or prepared pepper)

Three-dish Meals

Simple yam pottage	Green vegetable stew	Fried fish
Roasted yam or cocoyam	Roast fish or meat	Simple palm stew
Amala	Ewedu soup	Palm oil stew with dry fish or meat
Roast yam	Roast fresh fish	Simple leafy green stew
Boiled cowpeas	Boiled rice or yam	Simple palm oil stew with fish or meat
Frejon	Palm oil fish stew	Fine garri
Steamed cowpea paste (ekuru)	Simple palm oil stew	Eko, bread or rice
Pounded yam	Simple greens and egusi soup	Palm oil stew with beef and innards
Boiled ripe plantain	Rice	Palm oil stew with meat or fish
Rice	Fried ripe plantain (dodo)	Any palm oil stew with chicken, snails, beef or fresh fish
Boiled yam or ripe plantain	Roast fish or meat	Prepared peppered oil sauce
Eba	Sprats in groundnut oil stew	Simple leafy green vegetable stew
Boiled beans	Dry fine garri	Dry fish and crisp dry crayfish in palm oil
Shrimp coconut rice	Roast pork	Simple leafy green vegetable stew
Boiled yam	Simple herb sauce	Fried or roast meat, fish or chicken

For Weight-Watchers

With increasing reports of the ill effects of high blood pressure and obesity on health, many Nigerian men and women are seeking to control their waistlines. A friend who was convinced she could not lose weight claimed that she ate very little: 'just dodo and a little stew in the evening'. Plantain is a very high energy carbohydrate food; when fried, it becomes one of the most 'fattening' foods in our diet. Stews with oil, whether visible or emulsified, are also high in calories. Others are convinced that if they could cut down the water they drink, they would lose weight. Water has no calories and it is dangerous to cut down on its intake in our climate. These examples of ignorance about the causes for overweight are given to convince even the sceptic that he needs to be better informed about nutrition.

Briefly, let the slimmer, and the wife of the slimmer, improve his diet by increasing the amount of fruit and non-carbohydrate vegetables, white-fleshed fish and shellfish, and decreasing his intake of oily, fatty meats, fried foods, rice, garri, bread, yam and plantain and their products. It is expensive to diet, but it is more expensive to pay the price of being overweight.

If you are serious about losing weight, here are a few suggestions which may help:

1. Eat only at meal times. You may eat three small meals or five smaller ones.
2. Use a smaller plate than usual. Put the food you will eat on the plate in balanced portions and never have 'seconds'.
3. Wash your plate and leave the kitchen. Do not finish what is in the cooking pot or the children's left-overs.
4. Never have between-meal snacks. Keep yourself too busy to think about them.
5. Boil plantain, yam and other carbohydrate foods rather than frying them. Eat leafy green vegetable stews and okro soup rather than palm oil stews.
6. If you find your meals are not filling you up, have an orange, grapefruit or a large piece of pawpaw *before* eating your main meal. Your stomach will shrink after a few days and you will be satisfied with your plateful of food.
7. Drink plenty of water and avoid sweetened hot or cold beverages.
8. Weigh yourself twice a week at the same time of day.
9. Do more walking and take some regular strenuous exercise if you wish. For some people, exercise decreases the appetite; for others, it increases it.
10. When you have achieved your desired weight, continue eating small properly balanced meals. If you resume your old life style and bad eating habits, you will resume your old shape as well!

Glossary

Some of the difficulties in deciding on terminology were mentioned in Chapter 1. This glossary is intended to provide quick definitions and cross-references for terms in Nigerian languages and English as used in Nigeria and elsewhere.

Acha   Cereal grain used in northern part of Nigeria
Agidi   Eko
Akamu   Ogi; cooked fermented cornstarch
Akara   Fried cowpea paste fritters
Amala   Thickened carbohydrate prepared from yam flour
Apon   Ogbono
Awuje   Soft boiled cowpeas

Banga Soup   Soup prepared with palm fruit pulp
Beans   Common name for cowpeas
Beanflour   Name used commercially for cowpea flour
Benneseed   Sesame seed
'Black' Plantain or Banana   In markets refers to unripe green fruits
Blender   Liquidiser
Bush Meat   Meat from any undomesticated animal

Clarias (Claridae)   Scaleless fish with more than 40 varieties in Nigeria, ranging in size from very small to giant size. (Common name: mudfish. Yoruba: *aaro*).
Congo Meat   Land snail flesh
Cornflour   Cornstarch
Cowpeas   Proper name for what are called 'beans' in Nigeria
Crayfish   Common name in Nigeria for shrimps or prawns
Croaker   Sea fish ranging from small to giant sized, scaled
Cup   In markets 'cup' refers to a cup used to measure products; usually an evaporated milk tin. Previously a No 3 Players cigarette tin was most common. Today cups of various sizes are used, often partially filled with paper to decrease their volume, so always check before buying.

Dakua   Groundnut and maize snack food. See Chapter 10.
Dry Fish   See Chapter 5

Eba   Thickened carbohydrate food prepared from garri
Efo   General term for edible leafy greens (Yoruba)
Egusi   Dried shelled melon seeds (see Index)
Eko   Thickened cornstarch wrapped and cooled in leaves
Ekuru   Simple steamed cowpea paste
Evaporated Milk   Correct name for the term 'tinned milk' in Nigeria

Farina   Cassava product (See Chapter 3)
Fermented Starch   Starch removed from grain after soaking in water for some days; from maize, millet etc.
Fufu   This is a general term applied to most thickened carbohydrate foods. These may be prepared by pounding with yam, cocoyam and cassava, or from extracted starch such as cassava, or from ground whole grains such as millet, maize and rice. Most people use foofoo and fufu interchangeably.

Gbegiri   Cowpea-thickened stew
Ghee   Clarified butter (see Chapter 2)
Grapes   In Nigeria refers to grapefruit
Greens   Term used to refer to any edible leafy green vegetable in Nigeria
Groundnut   Peanut

Icefish   Nigerian term for any commercially frozen fish
Ikpekere   Thin slices of fried green plantain
Imoyo   Refers to dishes with a Brazilian influence introduced to Lagos by returning Africans in the last century
Ire   Large, edible grubs, widely consumed as a seasonal delicacy. (Yoruba)
Iru   Fermented locust bean
Isam   Periwinkles or small sea snails (Ibo)

Jero   Millet

Kaun   Potash
Kuka soup   Soup prepared with ground dry okro

Milk   Refers to whole cow's milk. Use fresh milk, reconstituted dried milk or 'tinned' (evaporated) milk diluted with water.

Mudu   Measuring container

Nuru   Dry okro (Okenne)

Ogbono   Apon
Ogi   Thickened fermented starch, particularly that made from maize
Ogi-baba   Thickened fermented millet starch

Peanuts   Groundnuts
Pears   In Nigeria refers to avocado pear
Pottage   Heavy stew thickened with boiled carbohydrate

'Red' Banana or Plantain   Often used in markets to describe the ripe yellow fruits

Small Chop   Finger food
Snails   Refers to land snails in Nigeria
Spinach   Refers in Nigeria to most edible leafy greens
Sweet   In Nigeria, if a food is 'sweet', it is tasty (not necessarily sweetened with sugar)
Sweets   Anything sweetened with sugar eaten as a snack e.g. candy, puddings, cakes etc.

Thickened Carbohydrate Food   This forms a firm mass and is generally eaten with fingers. The lumps of food are dipped into the soup or stew and then swallowed. These foods include eba, the various fufus, and tuwos. They can be made from roots, grains, cereals and fermented or unfermented starches derived from roots or grains
Tinned Fish   Fish in cans; usually mackerel or pilchards
Tinned Milk   Evaporated milk
Tinned Tomato   Canned tomato paste
Tomato Paste   Called tinned tomato in Nigeria
Tuwo   General term for thickened carbohydrate foods prepared by overcooking grains such as rice, millet, guinea corn etc.

Vegetable   In Nigeria 'vegetable' is usually used to refer to leafy green vegetables alone, although any edible part of any plant can be referred to as a vegetable.

Related Reading

Anazonwu-Bello, J.N., *Food and Nutrition in Practice*, Macmillan, 1976.

Dovlo, F.E., Williams, C.E., and Zoaka L, *Cowpeas: Home Preparation and Use in West Africa*, International Development Research Centre, 1976.

Holden, M and Reed, W, *West African Freshwater Fish*, Longman 1972.

Mars, J.A. and Tooleyo, E.M., *The Kudeti Book of Yoruba Cookery*, C.M.S. Bookshops, 1965.

Nyaho, E., Amarteifio, E., Asare, J, *Ghana Recipe Book*, Ghana Publishing Corporation, 1970.

Oyenuga, V.A., *Nigeria's Foods and Feeding-stuffs*, Ibadan University Press, 1968.

Ricketts, E., *Food, Health and You*, Macmillan 1966, Reprinted 1977.

Timitimi, A.O., *Izon fiai furn: Ijo Cookery Book*, Institute of African Studies, Univ: of Ibadan, Occasional Publications No. 28, 1970.

Vincent, A., *A Cookery Book for the Tropics*, Allen and Unwin, 1962 4th impression 1970.

Williams R.O., *Miss Williams' Cookery Book*, Longman 1957, 6th impression 1976.

Tables

1 Weights of common foodstuffs

Dry Foods

Food	Volume (Level Measure)	Weight (in grams)
Acha	1 mgt	200
African black pepper, whole	1 tsp	2
African nutmeg, shelled, ground	1 tsp. (3 seeds)	3
Agbono, whole, about 100 pieces	1 mt	83
whole, about 30 pieces	1 tpt	25
ground, packed	1 tpt	50
Cowpeas, dry whole	1 mgt	230
	1 mt	125
Cowpea flour	1 mgt	150
Cowpea paste	1 mgt	variable
Crayfish, dry, whole, small	1 mgt	50
dry, ground, loosely packed	1 tpt	20
dry, ground, pressed	1 tpt	40
dry, whole, large	1 mgt	45
Dry fish, medium size	as purchased	250
Egusi seeds, shelled	1 mt	95
ground, loosely packed	1 mt	70
ground, packed	1 mt	130
Farina	1 mt	80
Garri, dry	1 mgt	150
	1 mt	100
Granulated sugar	1 mt	156
Groundnuts, shelled	1 mgt	180-200
	1 mt	120-130
Fermented locust bean (iru)	1 dsp	10
Millet, guinea corn, maize, dry	1 mgt	225
	1 mt	125
meal	1 mgt	150
Okro, dry ground	1 tpt	40

TABLE 1 WEIGHTS OF COMMON FOODSTUFFS

Food	Volume (Level Measure)	Weight (in grams)
Pepper, dry red whole	1 mgt	75
ground	1 tsp	2
Potash, small piece	1 tsp	3
Rice, whole	1 mgt	200
ground	1 mgt	225
Wheat flour, white or brown	1 mt	125
	1 mgt	190

Fresh Foods

Food	Volume (Level Measure)	Weight (in grams)
Banana, small	1	75
large	1	200
mashed	1 mgt	225
1 medium, skinned and mashed	½ mt	100
Coconut, large	1	1.1 kg
small	1	400
grated, pressed down	1 mt	160
Cocoyam, medium	1	125
small	1	55
Eggs, large	1	70
small	1	55
Green leaves, market 'bundle'	1	150-300
chopped, pressed down	1 mgt	100
Meat	1 mt	200
	1 mgt	160
Ogi, wet (fermented cornstarch)	1 tpt	90
Okazi leaves, chopped, packed	1 mgt	125
Okro, large	3	54
small	3	25
Onion, 1 medium	1	150
1 large	1	270
chopped	1 tpt	50
Pepper, fresh red, ata rodo	1 med	3
tatasai	1 med	35
Pepper, fresh red, chopped	1 tpt	40
Palm fruits	2 congo	1.5 kg
Plantain, large	1	450
small	1	200
peeled, chopped	1 tpt	65
Shrimp	1 mt	150

Food	Volume (Level Measure)	Weight (in grams)
Snails, dressed	1 large	65
Starch, cassava	1 tpt	60
Sweet potato	1 medium	
Tomato	1 medium	90
	1 large	120
chopped	1 tpt	65
Yam	1 large	5 kg+
	1 small	1 kg
Slice: 2cm x 12 cm diameter	1	300
Boiled, mashed	1 tpt	40

2 Quick conversions

This table contains only those VOLUME quantitative measurements used regularly in this book; a more complete table of measurements and equivalents can be found in Table 3.

Part A

Abbreviations	Handy Measure (level)	Metric Equivalent
tsp	small teaspoon (British)	3 ml
dsp	dessertspoon (British)	9 ml
tpt	small tomato paste tin (70 g size)	70 ml
mt	small 'tinned milk' tin (170 g size)	190 ml
mgt	small margarine tin (225 g size); same volume as medium sized, 50g Nescafe tin	290 ml

Part B

Abbrevations	Handy Measure (level)	American Measures
pt	$1\frac{3}{4}$ mgt	pint (American, 16 oz)
c	$\frac{7}{8}$ mgt	cup (American, 8 oz)
	1 mgt	1 cup + 3 tablespoons
	1 mt	$\frac{7}{8}$ cup
	1 tpt	$\frac{1}{3}$ c
tblsp	$1\frac{1}{3}$ dsp	tablespoon (American)
	1 dsp	¾ t
t	$1\frac{1}{3}$ tsp (British size)	teaspoon (American)
	1 tsp (British size)	¾ t

Part C

Abbreviations	Handy Measure (level)	British Measures
pt	3½ mt	pint (British, 20 oz)
	1 mt	7 oz
	1 mgt	10½ oz
	1 tpt	2½ oz
dsp	dsp	dessertspoon
tsp	tsp	teaspoon (British)

3 Weight and volume conversions

Approximate equivalents useful for the recipes in this book.

Part 1 American Measures

American	British	Metric	Handy
1 gallon (4 qts)	$\frac{5}{6}$ gal.	4.2 l	1-1.2 'gallon' tins
1 quart (qt)	$\frac{5}{6}$ qt	1.05 l	1 Treetop btle + 1 mt
1 pint (pt)	$\frac{5}{6}$ pt	0.053	1 mgt + 1 mt or ¾ mgt
1 cup (c)	$\frac{5}{6}$ c	265 ml	$\frac{7}{8}$ mgt
1 tablespoon (tblsp)	$\frac{4}{5}$ tblsp	15 ml	$1\frac{1}{3}$ dsp
1 teaspoon (t)	$1\frac{1}{3}$ tsp	4.5 ml	$1\frac{1}{3}$ ts
1 pound (1b)	1 lb (16 oz)	454 g	
1 ounce (oz)	1 oz	30 g	

Part 2 Handy Measures

Handy Measure	British	Metric	American
'gallon' tin	3.75-4.5 l		
'congo'	52 oz	1.45 l	6½ c
cigarette cup	10 oz	280 ml	1¼ c
margarine tin (225 g size)	10½ oz	290 ml	1¼ c
milk tin	7 oz	190 ml	$\frac{7}{8}$ c
tomato paste tin (small 70 g size)	2½ oz	70 ml	$\frac{1}{3}$ c
'bottle'			
Treetop	25 oz	750 ml	$3\frac{1}{8}$ c
Lucozade	25½ oz	760 ml	$3\frac{1}{8}$ c
Beer (large)	18 oz	552 ml	2¼ c

Part 3 British Measures

British	Metric	Handy	American
gallon	5.1	'gallon' tin (large)	20 c (1.2 gal)
quart	1.2 l	4 mgt	5 c
pint	600 ml	2 mgt	2½ c
teacup	300 ml	1 mgt	1¼ c
dessertspoon	9 ml	1 dsp.	$\frac{3}{4}$ tblsp
teaspoon	3 ml	1 tsp.	¾ c
tablespoon	19 ml	2 dsp.	1¼ tblsp

Part 4 Metric Measures

Metric	British	American
litre (l)	33 oz	$4\frac{1}{8}$ c
kilogram (kg)	2.2 lb	2.2 lb
gram (g)	0.035 oz	0.035 oz

Index

Acha, 30
Agbono, 101, 108-10, 150-1
Avocado pear, 146

Baking tins, 9
Banana, 52-5; cake, 183; fritters, 166; leaves, 121
Banga soup, 73, 79, 84, 98, 103-5
Beef, 68, 72-6, 172
Beverages, 175-6
Biscuits, 178-82
Bitter leaf, 135; stew, 139
Blancmange, 186-7
Blender, 10
Bottles, airtight, 8
Breads, 189-95
Breakfast, 200-1
Bush-meat, 69, 79

Cakes, 182-4
Can opener, 9
Cassava, 30-4, 179-80, 182-3
Cheese dishes, 156
Chicken, 81-6
Chin-chin, 179
Chopping-boards, 6-7
Coconut, 188; biscuits, 178-81; bread, 189; cake, 182-3; candy, 184-5; rice, 122; soups, 154
Cocoyam, 34-6, 100-1
Cole slaw, 145
Cornstarch, 50-1, 185-7
Cowpeas, 37-47, 74, 165, 170-1; soup, 75, 114, 149; spread, 174; stew, 39, 117-18; tea cake, 190
Crabs, 94, 125-6
Crayfish, 94, 105, 107-113, 172
Creme caramel, 188
Cucumber, 144
Curries, 85-6, 159, 173
Custards, 185-7

Deep freeze, 9
Deep fryer, 10
Doughnut balls, 178

Efo soup, 74
Egg: bread, 193; dishes, 156-9
Egusi, 26-7, 45, 108-9, 167; soup, 76-7, 82-3, 111, 130-1, 140
Equipment: modern, 5-9; traditional, 4-5
Ewedu, 135; soup, 137

Farina porridge, 186
Fish: dry, 90-2, 98, 100-17, 130-1; fresh, 88-90, 96-100; frozen, 90; paté, 174; recipes, 95-126
Flavourings, miscellaneous, 16, 21-2
Foodgrinder, 10
Frejon, 40-1
Fruit squashes, fresh, 176
Fruits, 195-7

Ghanaian dodo, 168
Ginger beer, 176
Goat meat, 68-70, 79-81, 172
Granola, 171
Graters, 7
Grinding stone, 5
Groundnuts and groundnut oil, 27, 103, 113-14, 162-5; biscuits, 181; butter, 163; stew, 72, 76, 95, 96, 113-14, 148
Guavas, 196-7; jam, 198
Guinea corn, 47-8; flour, 195

Herbs, 16, 20-1

Imoyo: chicken, 84-5; eba, 32-3; eleja, 96-7
Insects, fried, 172

Jams, 197-8
Jars, airtight, 8

Kitchens: modern, 3-4; traditional, 2-3
Knives, 7-8

Larvae, fried, 172
Lemon curd filling, 184
Light meals, 200-1

INDEX

Liver, 69, 76–7, 172
Locust bean stew, 101, 141

Main meals, 201–4
Maize, 33–4, 49–50, 163–6; meal, 52; pudding, 51
Measuring containers, standard, 8–9
Meat, 68–71; recipes, 71–81
Milk dishes, 156
Millet, 47–9; flour, 49, 195; soup, 149
Mortar and pestle, 4–5
Moyin — moyin, 44–5

Oil bean salad, 142
Oils and fats, 16, 22–5
Okazi soup, 118–19
Okro, 75, 136, 140–1; soup, 74–5, 98, 103, 108, 123, 152
Omelette, 158
One-dish meals, 201–2
Orange bread, 191

Palm oil, 23–4, 36, 107: stew, 72, 96, 110, 148–9
Pawpaw: jam, 198; muffins, 191–2
Peanut butter, 163
Periwinkles, 94, 120
Pineapple: ice, 197; jam, 198
Plantain, 53–5, 80, 167–9, 188; loaf, 190–1; pottage, 38, 77–9, 115–17, 130; pudding, 55
Pork, 68, 77–9
Porridge, 185–6
Pots and pans, 5, 6; holders, 8
Poultry, 81–6
Prawns, 94, 99–100, 119–20
Pressure cooker, 9
Pumpkins, fluted, 135, 171

Recipes, use of, 11–12
Red peppers, 16, 19; soup, 150
Refrigerator, 9
Rice, 55–9, 122–4; bread, 189–91; ground, 58–9; jollof, 56–7, 86; pudding, 186

Salads, 142–6; dressing, 144–5
Sandwich spreads, 173–5
Sauces, 151, 153
Seeds, 25–8
Semovita eba, 61
Sheep meat, 68–9
Shellfish, 94
Shrimps, 119–25
Sieves, 7
Skillet, 6
Snails, 110, 128–32, 172
Sorghum, 47–8
Soups, 149–54; packet, 153–4
Spices, seed and root, 16–19
Sponge cake, 183–4
Spoons, 7
Sprats, 94–5
Steamer, 6
Stews, 148–9
Stockfish, 92, 94, 117–18, 139
Stoves, 5–6
Suya, 172
Sweet potato, 59

Three-dish meals, 204
Tins, airtight, 8
Tomato, 143–4
Towels and towel rod, 8
Two-dish meals, 202–3

Vegetables: green, 134–7; other, 137; recipes using, 137–41

Wateryam, 59–60; pottage, 116; soup, 105–6
Weight watching, 204–5
Weights and measures, 12–14
Wheat, 60–1
Whitebait, 94–5

Yam, 62–5, 77, 80; pottage, 64–5, 105
Yeast rolls, 195
Yoghurt, 159–60